Becoming A Vessel
GOD CAN USE

Prayer
Journal

Bethany House Books
by Donna Partow

Becoming a Vessel God Can Use
Becoming a Vessel God Can Use AudioBook
Living in Absolute Freedom
Walking in Total God-Confidence
Standing Firm
A Woman's Guide to Personality Types

DONNA PARTOW is a Christian communicator with a compelling testimony of God's transforming power. From her childhood as "the kid no one was allowed to play with" to her days as a drug dealer and her marriage to a strict Middle Eastern husband, she shares her life journey with disarming honesty and humor.

Donna's uncommon transparency and passion for Christ have been used by God at women's conferences and retreats around the country. She has been a popular guest on more than 200 radio and TV programs, including *Focus on the Family.*

She is the bestselling author of numerous books including *Becoming a Vessel God Can Use.*

If your church sponsors an annual women's retreat, perhaps they would be interested in learning more about Donna's special weekend program. For more information Donna can be reached by email at: donnapartow@cybertrails.com or through her Web site: *donnapartow.com*

Becoming A Vessel
GOD CAN USE

Prayer Journal

A Guided Devotional Journey by

Donna Partow

BETHANY HOUSE
Minneapolis, Minnesota

Published by Bethany House Publishers
A Ministry of Bethany Fellowship International
11400 Hampshire Avenue South
Bloomington, Minnesota 55438
www.bethanyhouse.com

Printed in China

Library of Congress Cataloging-in-Publication Data

Partow, Donna.
    Becoming a vessel God can use prayer journal
        p. cm.
    ISBN 0-7642-2669-X
    1. Christian women—Religious life. 2. Spiritual journals—Authorship.
I. Title.
    BV4527 .P37 2002
    248.8'43—dc20

                                                            2002002716

Introduction

Do I have to be perfect?

As you begin this devotional journey, the exciting truth I want you to grab hold of is this: God can use imperfect vessels like you and me. In fact, he often delights in choosing the most unlikely people to accomplish his purposes in this world. Everyone around you may consider you the least likely job candidate, but fortunately, God works as his own employment recruiter! No matter who you are, if you will yield your life to God, you can become a vessel God can use.

I urge you to set aside time *daily* to concentrate on your relationship with your heavenly Father. I hope you will make time with God a genuine priority in your life. The housecleaning will wait; someone else can bake the brownies for a while; your favorite TV shows aren't *that* important. Nevertheless, hectic days will come. If you can't journal daily, make it a weekly time that takes priority over other activities—perhaps on Sunday afternoon or evening.

As you begin your devotional time, spend a few moments focusing on God, asking him to show you what he has for you today. Read and reread the Scripture, my reflections, and the questions (they're the same every day—to help you focus). Then be quiet before him—listen. Write whatever the Holy Spirit brings to mind; write your questions to God. There are no right or wrong answers. No one will grade your paper. This is your private conversation with God.

Because you may write things that only God should see, keep your journal in a private place: in your undies drawer, on top of the refrigerator, or stashed under the bed. Just don't hide it so well that you forget where it is or to use it!

Keeping a spiritual journal won't make you perfect and it isn't easy, but I promise you will gain a fuller understanding of the price and possibilities, the challenges and the joys of *Becoming a Vessel God Can Use*.

Five Requirements for Becoming
A Vessel God Can Use

ACCEPT
the way God made you.

Be *EMPTIED* of self
to make room for God.

Allow God to *CLEANSE* you
even if the process is painful.

Be *FILLED* and constantly refilled
with the Living Water of the Holy Spirit.

POUR OUT your life
in ministry *as God directs*.

[Sisters], think of what you were when you were called. Not many of you were wise by human standards; not many were influential; not many were of noble birth. But God chose the foolish things of the world to shame the wise; God chose the weak things of the world to shame the strong. He chose the lowly things of this world and the despised things—and the things that are not—to nullify the things that are, so that no one may boast before him. It is because of him that you are in Christ Jesus, who has become for us wisdom from God—that is, our righteousness, holiness and redemption. Therefore, as it is written: "Let him who boasts boast in the Lord."

1 CORINTHIANS 1:26–31

What is God calling you to ACCEPT today?

Motherhood – Not letting confrontation break my Spirit being fair + honest with my children + husband

What is God calling you to be EMPTIED of, in order to make room for him? Is it something painful from your past, your agenda for today, or something you dream of for tomorrow?

Anger, Jelousy.
I need to stop becoming so angry when the children argue with me. I'm not being a good example of how to act.

What do you need to be CLEANSED of today? Reflect and confess any known sin; ask God to reveal any areas that need cleansing.

I'm sorry for yelling @ my children.
I wish I had more patients when it comes to confrontation. I need to step back, take a deep breath + be the adult. My children will never know how to discuss things calmly if I don't show them. I need to be the example.

How is your life demonstrating the FILLING of the Holy Spirit?
How can you actively BE FILLED today?

How is God directing you to POUR FORTH in ministry today?
Who has he laid on your heart?

I'm trying to have my children think and pray to God. It reminds me to follow in his word also. If they can think about praying and God's Word more, it will calm them and help them make better choices. I need to be the example.

As I studied my Bible, determined to uncover what the heroes of the Bible had in common, I discovered a collection of the most unlikely people imaginable. From homemakers and prophets to prostitutes and murderers, God was able to work through anyone who firmly believed he could and would use imperfect vessels. As I have gradually released my own agenda and turned myself over to God—broken, imperfect vessel that I am—he has begun to work through my life.

For the foolishness of God is wiser than man's wisdom,
and the weakness of God is stronger than man's strength.
1 CORINTHIANS 1: 25

What is God calling you to ACCEPT today?

I need to speak freely, not push everything down inside me. I need to deal with things as they come up. + not dismise my feelings. I need to learn to communicate my feelings + recieve feedback w/out feeling attacked.

What is God calling you to be EMPTIED of, in order to make room for him? Is it something painful from your past, your agenda for today, or something you dream of for tomorrow?

Embarrasment. feeling like my problems arent important. I just want a healthy relationship. Were we can talk about anything + everything.

What do you need to be CLEANSED of today? Reflect and confess any known sin; ask God to reveal any areas that need cleansing.

I need to be more understanding. Not have such negative thoughts. I need to open up my heart + my mind to other opinions.

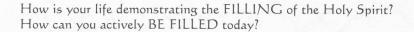

How is your life demonstrating the FILLING of the Holy Spirit? How can you actively BE FILLED today?

How is God directing you to POUR FORTH in ministry today? Who has he laid on your heart?

God can use imperfect vessels like you and me. In fact, he often delights in choosing the most unlikely people to accomplish his purposes in this world. Everyone around you may consider you the least likely job candidate, but fortunately God works as his own employment recruiter! No matter who you are, if you will yield your life to God you can become a vessel God can use.

Since you are precious and honored in my sight, and because I love you, I will give men in exchange for you, and people in exchange for your life.
ISAIAH 43:4

What is God calling you to ACCEPT today?

That I will not have any more Children.

What is God calling you to be EMPTIED of, in order to make room for him? Is it something painful from your past, your agenda for today, or something you dream of for tomorrow?

What do you need to be CLEANSED of today? Reflect and confess any known sin; ask God to reveal any areas that need cleansing.

How is your life demonstrating the FILLING of the Holy Spirit? How can you actively BE FILLED today?

How is God directing you to POUR FORTH in ministry today? Who has he laid on your heart?

Maybe when you think about the kind of vessel you are, words like *chipped, cracked, broken,* and *dirty* come to mind. Maybe you feel like a dusty old jar forgotten on the shelf or an ugly water jug abandoned by the side of the road. Maybe you see yourself as a crystal vase—you look good from a distance, and people admire you—but a closer look reveals cracks from top to bottom. What matters is not how you see yourself but how God sees you. He created you and he has a plan.

For I know the plans I have for you," declares the Lord, "plans to prosper you and not to harm you, plans to give you hope and a future. Then you will call upon me and come and pray to me, and I will listen to you. You will seek me and find me when you seek me with all your heart."

JEREMIAH 29:11–13

What is God calling you to ACCEPT today?

What is God calling you to be EMPTIED of, in order to make room for him? Is it something painful from your past, your agenda for today, or something you dream of for tomorrow?

What do you need to be CLEANSED of today? Reflect and confess any known sin; ask God to reveal any areas that need cleansing.

How is your life demonstrating the FILLING of the Holy Spirit?
How can you actively BE FILLED today?

How is God directing you to POUR FORTH in ministry today?
Who has he laid on your heart?

When I became a Christian I had very clear ideas about
what my gifts were and how I could be useful to God. God
had done so much for me that I wanted to do things for him
in return. Unfortunately my focus was on myself and the
great things I was going to accomplish for God rather than
on God and the great things he wants to accomplish through
me. God created you with a specific plan in mind, which will
unfold when you yield your life to him.

All the days ordained for me were written in your book before one of them came to be.
PSALM 139:16

What is God calling you to ACCEPT today?

What is God calling you to be EMPTIED of, in order to make room for him? Is it something painful from your past, your agenda for today, or something you dream of for tomorrow?

What do you need to be CLEANSED of today? Reflect and confess any known sin; ask God to reveal any areas that need cleansing.

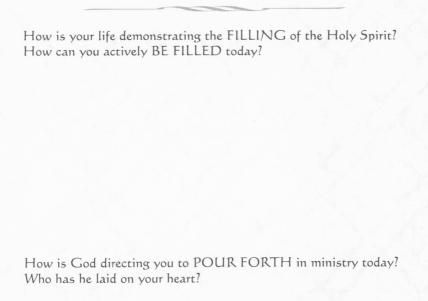

How is your life demonstrating the FILLING of the Holy Spirit? How can you actively BE FILLED today?

How is God directing you to POUR FORTH in ministry today? Who has he laid on your heart?

Understanding what God wants to accomplish through your life is far more important than deciding what you think you can accomplish for him. Accept the purpose for which God created you, even if it's not the life you envisioned for yourself.

Come to me, all you who are weary and burdened, and I will give you rest. Take my yoke upon you and learn from me, for I am gentle and humble in heart, and you will find rest for your souls. For my yoke is easy and my burden is light."
MATTHEW 11:28–30

What is God calling you to ACCEPT today?

What is God calling you to be EMPTIED of, in order to make room for him? Is it something painful from your past, your agenda for today, or something you dream of for tomorrow?

What do you need to be CLEANSED of today? Reflect and confess any known sin; ask God to reveal any areas that need cleansing.

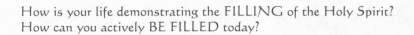

How is your life demonstrating the FILLING of the Holy Spirit? How can you actively BE FILLED today?

How is God directing you to POUR FORTH in ministry today? Who has he laid on your heart?

As you learn to become a moldable, usable vessel in the hands of God, you'll discover that ministry is no longer a burden, no longer a list of things you have to do. Rather, it's a simple matter of listening for God's voice and then following where he leads.

To obey is *better than sacrifice.*
1 SAMUEL 15:22

What is God calling you to ACCEPT today?

What is God calling you to be EMPTIED of, in order to make room for him? Is it something painful from your past, your agenda for today, or something you dream of for tomorrow?

What do you need to be CLEANSED of today? Reflect and confess any known sin; ask God to reveal any areas that need cleansing.

How is your life demonstrating the FILLING of the Holy Spirit?
How can you actively BE FILLED today?

How is God directing you to POUR FORTH in ministry today?
Who has he laid on your heart?

God isn't interested in our excuses. There's no need for us to
waste God's time pointing out our weaknesses or the obstacles we face. He knows our circumstances far better than we
do ourselves. God knows you fully and he knows what you
are capable of doing through the power of the Holy Spirit.
He will only call you to complete a job he knows you can
handle with His power. When God calls us to obey, all he
wants is our obedience; he'll handle the details.

We all stumble in many ways.
JAMES 3:2

What is God calling you to ACCEPT today?

What is God calling you to be EMPTIED of, in order to make room for him? Is it something painful from your past, your agenda for today, or something you dream of for tomorrow?

What do you need to be CLEANSED of today? Reflect and confess any known sin; ask God to reveal any areas that need cleansing.

How is your life demonstrating the FILLING of the Holy Spirit? How can you actively BE FILLED today?

How is God directing you to POUR FORTH in ministry today? Who has he laid on your heart?

Even when we stumble and fall, God can still use us, because our lives become a warning to others that we are all vulnerable to Satan's attack. When we turn our hearts back to him, we can know with confidence that God will restore us.

For my thoughts are not your thoughts, neither are your ways my ways," declares the Lord. "As the heavens are higher than the earth, so are my ways higher than your ways and my thoughts than your thoughts."
ISAIAH 55:8–9

What is God calling you to ACCEPT today?

What is God calling you to be EMPTIED of, in order to make room for him? Is it something painful from your past, your agenda for today, or something you dream of for tomorrow?

What do you need to be CLEANSED of today? Reflect and confess any known sin; ask God to reveal any areas that need cleansing.

How is your life demonstrating the FILLING of the Holy Spirit? How can you actively BE FILLED today?

How is God directing you to POUR FORTH in ministry today? Who has he laid on your heart?

In choosing the most unlikely vessels to accomplish his work—something the world would consider foolish—God shows that even his seemingly foolish ideas are wiser than man's wisdom. When people behold something only God can do—like getting the job done through imperfect people—their eyes turn heavenward. God receives the glory due him and man is restored to a right relationship with his Creator.

For the eyes of the Lord range throughout the earth to strengthen those whose hearts are fully committed to him.
2 CHRONICLES 16:9

What is God calling you to ACCEPT today?

What is God calling you to be EMPTIED of, in order to make room for him? Is it something painful from your past, your agenda for today, or something you dream of for tomorrow?

What do you need to be CLEANSED of today? Reflect and confess any known sin; ask God to reveal any areas that need cleansing.

How is your life demonstrating the FILLING of the Holy Spirit?
How can you actively BE FILLED today?

How is God directing you to POUR FORTH in ministry today?
Who has he laid on your heart?

Self-confidence is often a major hindrance to becoming a vessel God can use, because it is based on trust in your own ability to handle people and circumstances. God-confidence is trust in God's ability to work through you, regardless of your natural abilities. With God-confidence, you can forget about your own strengths and weaknesses, knowing that God can get the job done, regardless. With God-confidence, you are freed from both pride and self-recrimination. You can focus on the job at hand and on the needs of others, leaving the results with God, where they belong.

His master replied, *"Well done, good and faithful servant! You have been faithful with a few things; I will put you in charge of many things. Come and share your master's happiness!"*
MATTHEW 25:21

What is God calling you to ACCEPT today?

What is God calling you to be EMPTIED of, in order to make room for him? Is it something painful from your past, your agenda for today, or something you dream of for tomorrow?

What do you need to be CLEANSED of today? Reflect and confess any known sin; ask God to reveal any areas that need cleansing.

How is your life demonstrating the FILLING of the Holy Spirit?
How can you actively BE FILLED today?

How is God directing you to POUR FORTH in ministry today?
Who has he laid on your heart?

Far better to accomplish one thing—touch one life—for eternity, by serving as a vessel God can use, than to accomplish great things by the world's standards, only to earn the applause of men. Which matters more to you: temporary results or eternal rewards?

If any man builds on this foundation using gold, silver, costly stones, wood, hay or straw, his work will be shown for what it is, because the Day will bring it to light. It will be revealed with fire, and the fire will test the quality of each man's work. If what he has built survives, he will receive his reward. If it is burned up, he will suffer loss; he himself will be saved, but only as one escaping through the flames.

1 Corinthians 3:12–15

What is God calling you to ACCEPT today?

What is God calling you to be EMPTIED of, in order to make room for him? Is it something painful from your past, your agenda for today, or something you dream of for tomorrow?

What do you need to be CLEANSED of today? Reflect and confess any known sin; ask God to reveal any areas that need cleansing.

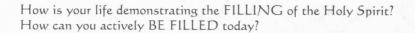

How is your life demonstrating the FILLING of the Holy Spirit? How can you actively BE FILLED today?

How is God directing you to POUR FORTH in ministry today? Who has he laid on your heart?

It will be a fearful moment for men who've built huge churches on personal charisma when they stand before the throne and God says their impressive numbers are just so much hay and stubble. What a joyous moment for the humble housewife who quietly ministered to the women of her neighborhood because she did it for God's glory and by his power. Her reward will be great.

Moses answered the people, "Do not be afraid. Stand firm and you will see the deliverance the Lord will bring you today. The Egyptians you see today you will never see again. The Lord will fight for you; you need only to be still."
EXODUS 14:13–14

What is God calling you to ACCEPT today?

What is God calling you to be EMPTIED of, in order to make room for him? Is it something painful from your past, your agenda for today, or something you dream of for tomorrow?

What do you need to be CLEANSED of today? Reflect and confess any known sin; ask God to reveal any areas that need cleansing.

How is your life demonstrating the FILLING of the Holy Spirit? How can you actively BE FILLED today?

How is God directing you to POUR FORTH in ministry today? Who has he laid on your heart?

When we rely on ourselves or look for mere human solutions—forgetting about the God factor—we act foolishly. As a result of our proud attitude, we end up at war with the people around us. Why are we so prone to look to ourselves and our own resources when God delights in putting his resources to work on our behalf? When we place our confidence in God and God alone, he promises to strengthen us and to fight on our behalf. That's the best battle plan of all.

Therefore, if anyone is in Christ, he is a new creation; the old has gone, the new has come!
2 CORINTHIANS 5:17

What is God calling you to ACCEPT today?

What is God calling you to be EMPTIED of, in order to make room for him? Is it something painful from your past, your agenda for today, or something you dream of for tomorrow?

What do you need to be CLEANSED of today? Reflect and confess any known sin; ask God to reveal any areas that need cleansing.

How is your life demonstrating the FILLING of the Holy Spirit?
How can you actively BE FILLED today?

How is God directing you to POUR FORTH in ministry today?
Who has he laid on your heart?

A person's career does not tell the whole story about who she
is. The most unlikely people can demonstrate character, cour-
age, and faith. Don't let anyone judge you by what you do;
what matters is who you are in Christ.

Therefore, I urge you, *[sisters]*, *in view of God's mercy,* *to offer your bodies as living sacrifices, holy and pleasing to God—* *this is your spiritual act of worship. Do not conform any longer to the* *pattern of this world, but be transformed by the renewing of your* *mind. Then you will be able to test and approve what God's will is—* *his good, pleasing and perfect will.*
ROMANS 12:1–2

What is God calling you to ACCEPT today?

What is God calling you to be EMPTIED of, in order to make room for him? Is it something painful from your past, your agenda for today, or something you dream of for tomorrow?

What do you need to be CLEANSED of today? Reflect and confess any known sin; ask God to reveal any areas that need cleansing.

How is your life demonstrating the FILLING of the Holy Spirit?
How can you actively BE FILLED today?

How is God directing you to POUR FORTH in ministry today?
Who has he laid on your heart?

Can you think of even one area in your life where you are
going against the crowd? If not, perhaps you are being conformed to this world, rather than being transformed by the
renewing of your mind.

In the same way, was not even Rahab the prostitute considered righteous for what she did when she gave lodging to the spies and sent them off in a different direction?
JAMES 2:25

What is God calling you to ACCEPT today?

What is God calling you to be EMPTIED of, in order to make room for him? Is it something painful from your past, your agenda for today, or something you dream of for tomorrow?

What do you need to be CLEANSED of today? Reflect and confess any known sin; ask God to reveal any areas that need cleansing.

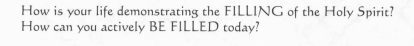

How is your life demonstrating the FILLING of the Holy Spirit? How can you actively BE FILLED today?

How is God directing you to POUR FORTH in ministry today? Who has he laid on your heart?

Will you dare to believe that God can use you, regardless of your past? Rahab did, and she was commended for it. When you depend on God alone—accepting your life just as you have lived it and allowing him to empty you of the pain of the past—there is no limit to what God can accomplish in and through your life.

We are therefore Christ's ambassadors, as though God were *making his appeal through us.*
2 CORINTHIANS 5:20

What is God calling you to ACCEPT today?

What is God calling you to be EMPTIED of, in order to make room for him? Is it something painful from your past, your agenda for today, or something you dream of for tomorrow?

What do you need to be CLEANSED of today? Reflect and confess any known sin; ask God to reveal any areas that need cleansing.

How is your life demonstrating the FILLING of the Holy Spirit?
How can you actively BE FILLED today?

How is God directing you to POUR FORTH in ministry today?
Who has he laid on your heart?

We all wear labels that either help or hinder God's work in
our lives. Old labels don't have to control our future, but if
we let them, they can do incredible damage. Remember this:
Don't let what you used to be prevent you from becoming
what you ought to be. What you ought to be—what in fact
you already are, whether you live out that calling or not—is
Christ's ambassador.

Yet to all who received him, to those who believed in his name, he gave the right to become children of God.
JOHN 1:12

What is God calling you to ACCEPT today?

What is God calling you to be EMPTIED of, in order to make room for him? Is it something painful from your past, your agenda for today, or something you dream of for tomorrow?

What do you need to be CLEANSED of today? Reflect and confess any known sin; ask God to reveal any areas that need cleansing.

How is your life demonstrating the FILLING of the Holy Spirit? How can you actively BE FILLED today?

How is God directing you to POUR FORTH in ministry today? Who has he laid on your heart?

Have you been labeled? Maybe a parent, a teacher, or other children put a label on you that you can't seem to shake— *Suzie Stupid, Fat Phyllis*. Or maybe it's something more recent. Maybe you feel like you've blown it too many times: in your marriage, in your neighborhood, at your job, or in your church. They've labeled you a lousy Christian; and frankly, you feel like the label fits. God wants to remove all your old labels and replace them with a new one: Daughter of the King.

There is no one like the God of Jeshurun, who rides on the heavens to help you and on the clouds in his majesty. The eternal God is your refuge, and underneath are the everlasting arms.
DEUTERONOMY 33:26–27

What is God calling you to ACCEPT today?

What is God calling you to be EMPTIED of, in order to make room for him? Is it something painful from your past, your agenda for today, or something you dream of for tomorrow?

What do you need to be CLEANSED of today? Reflect and confess any known sin; ask God to reveal any areas that need cleansing.

How is your life demonstrating the FILLING of the Holy Spirit? How can you actively BE FILLED today?

How is God directing you to POUR FORTH in ministry today? Who has he laid on your heart?

When you blow it (and we all blow it sometimes), God comes to the rescue. He "rides on the heavens to help you." With his "everlasting arms" he stands ready to catch you. The very one who "rides on the clouds in his majesty" is the one who bends down to pick up the broken pieces of your life. He's the One who gently glues the pieces back together and returns you to a place of being a vessel he can use.

For everyone born of God overcomes the world. This is the victory that has overcome the world, even our faith. Who is it that overcomes the world? Only he who believes that Jesus is the Son of God.

     1 JOHN 5:4–5

What is God calling you to ACCEPT today?

What is God calling you to be EMPTIED of, in order to make room for him? Is it something painful from your past, your agenda for today, or something you dream of for tomorrow?

What do you need to be CLEANSED of today? Reflect and confess any known sin; ask God to reveal any areas that need cleansing.

How is your life demonstrating the FILLING of the Holy Spirit?
How can you actively BE FILLED today?

How is God directing you to POUR FORTH in ministry today?
Who has he laid on your heart?

There's no such thing as a vessel God can't do without.
There's not a human being on earth God *needs*. Sometimes I
think we imagine God as a nervous baseball coach, sitting on
the sidelines during the ninth inning—pacing the dugout
helplessly, wringing his hands and hoping his team can pull
off a last-minute victory. Nothing could be further from the
truth! He knows the end from the beginning. The victory is
assured. All we need to do is believe. Doesn't that take the
pressure off?

Observe therefore all the commands I am giving you today, so that you may have the strength to go in and take over the land that you are crossing the Jordan to possess, and so that you may live long in the land that the Lord swore to your forefathers to give to them and their descendants, a land flowing with milk and honey.
DEUTERONOMY 11: 8–9

What is God calling you to ACCEPT today?

What is God calling you to be EMPTIED of, in order to make room for him? Is it something painful from your past, your agenda for today, or something you dream of for tomorrow?

What do you need to be CLEANSED of today? Reflect and confess any known sin; ask God to reveal any areas that need cleansing.

How is your life demonstrating the FILLING of the Holy Spirit? How can you actively BE FILLED today?

How is God directing you to POUR FORTH in ministry today? Who has he laid on your heart?

When you understand who the potter is, when you understand the power and majesty of the God you serve, you will realize how little you need to do—and how much you need to yield, how much you need to trust, how much you need to humbly obey. God wants to give you good things, but like any reasonable parent, our Father gives good gifts to obedient children.

Who among the gods is like you, O Lord? Who is like you—majestic in holiness, awesome in glory, working wonders? In your unfailing love you will lead the people you have redeemed.
EXODUS 15:11, 13

What is God calling you to ACCEPT today?

What is God calling you to be EMPTIED of, in order to make room for him? Is it something painful from your past, your agenda for today, or something you dream of for tomorrow?

What do you need to be CLEANSED of today? Reflect and confess any known sin; ask God to reveal any areas that need cleansing.

How is your life demonstrating the FILLING of the Holy Spirit? How can you actively BE FILLED today?

How is God directing you to POUR FORTH in ministry today? Who has he laid on your heart?

God has redeemed you, and because you know you are redeemed, you can rest in the promise that he will lead you. Even when you can't see where you're going, even when nothing in your life makes sense, you can entrust yourself to your majestic God, knowing that in his unfailing love, he will lead the people he has redeemed. And that includes you.

Yours, O Lord, is the greatness and the power and the glory and the majesty and the splendor, for everything in heaven and earth is yours. Yours, O Lord, is the kingdom; you are exalted as head over all.

1 CHRONICLES 29:11

What is God calling you to ACCEPT today?

What is God calling you to be EMPTIED of, in order to make room for him? Is it something painful from your past, your agenda for today, or something you dream of for tomorrow?

What do you need to be CLEANSED of today? Reflect and confess any known sin; ask God to reveal any areas that need cleansing.

How is your life demonstrating the FILLING of the Holy Spirit?
How can you actively BE FILLED today?

How is God directing you to POUR FORTH in ministry today?
Who has he laid on your heart?

If we really understood the character of our God, we would
run to him. Like a child, we would skip and hop to him.
Instead of running to God, we often run to people. The truth
is, even the most noble person will fail us; even the most
well-intentioned, spiritual friend doesn't possess the wisdom
and character of God. The next time you face a crisis,
remember: you can take it to the throne or to the phone!
Which will you choose?

The Lord reigns, he is robed in majesty; the Lord is robed in majesty and is armed with strength. The world is firmly established; it cannot be moved.

PSALM 93:1

What is God calling you to ACCEPT today?

What is God calling you to be EMPTIED of, in order to make room for him? Is it something painful from your past, your agenda for today, or something you dream of for tomorrow?

What do you need to be CLEANSED of today? Reflect and confess any known sin; ask God to reveal any areas that need cleansing.

How is your life demonstrating the FILLING of the Holy Spirit? How can you actively BE FILLED today?

How is God directing you to POUR FORTH in ministry today? Who has he laid on your heart?

Our God is an awesome God! When we behold the majesty and goodness of our God, it should inspire us to want to know him more. What has been your attitude toward God? Toward learning his Word and spending time in prayer? Has it been a sense of duty? Or have you truly taken delight in his presence? Examine your heart before him.

Let us then approach the throne of grace with confidence, so that we may receive mercy and find grace to help us in our time of need.
HEBREWS 4:16

What is God calling you to ACCEPT today?

What is God calling you to be EMPTIED of, in order to make room for him? Is it something painful from your past, your agenda for today, or something you dream of for tomorrow?

What do you need to be CLEANSED of today? Reflect and confess any known sin; ask God to reveal any areas that need cleansing.

How is your life demonstrating the FILLING of the Holy Spirit? How can you actively BE FILLED today?

How is God directing you to POUR FORTH in ministry today? Who has he laid on your heart?

Isn't it wonderful to know God will never give us the cold shoulder? We can approach the very throne of the God of the Universe. As his children, we walk into his presence with full confidence, knowing he will receive us with loving, open arms. How can we not delight in that? How can we list that on our "things to do today" as if we needed to be reminded?

He gathers the lambs in his arms and carries them close to his heart; he gently leads those that have young.
ISAIAH 40:11

What is God calling you to ACCEPT today?

What is God calling you to be EMPTIED of, in order to make room for him? Is it something painful from your past, your agenda for today, or something you dream of for tomorrow?

What do you need to be CLEANSED of today? Reflect and confess any known sin; ask God to reveal any areas that need cleansing.

How is your life demonstrating the FILLING of the Holy Spirit?
How can you actively BE FILLED today?

How is God directing you to POUR FORTH in ministry today?
Who has he laid on your heart?

I remember taking my daughter Leah to Disneyland. When
she saw a performer dressed up like Beauty (from *Beauty and
the Beast*), she was overjoyed. I thought she was going to
leap out of her skin. Now think about it: she could not con-
tain her excitement in the presence of a twenty-something
girl dressed up like a fictional, animated character. How much
more should we delight in the presence of God, allowing him
to gather and lead us like little ones?

The sovereign Lord comes with power, and his arm rules for him.
ISAIAH 40:10

What is God calling you to ACCEPT today?

What is God calling you to be EMPTIED of, in order to make room for him? Is it something painful from your past, your agenda for today, or something you dream of for tomorrow?

What do you need to be CLEANSED of today? Reflect and confess any known sin; ask God to reveal any areas that need cleansing.

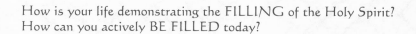

How is your life demonstrating the FILLING of the Holy Spirit?
How can you actively BE FILLED today?

How is God directing you to POUR FORTH in ministry today?
Who has he laid on your heart?

As we behold God's power and majesty, it becomes abundantly clear: God does not *need* you or me or anyone else. He rules the world with all power and authority. Yet He chooses to give us the privilege of joining him in his work. God is not looking for heroes. Just empty vessels.

For those God foreknew he also predestined to be conformed to the likeness of his Son, that he might be the firstborn among many brothers. And those he predestined, he also called; those he called, he also justified; those he justified, he also glorified.
ROMANS 8:29–30

What is God calling you to ACCEPT today?

What is God calling you to be EMPTIED of, in order to make room for him? Is it something painful from your past, your agenda for today, or something you dream of for tomorrow?

What do you need to be CLEANSED of today? Reflect and confess any known sin; ask God to reveal any areas that need cleansing.

How is your life demonstrating the FILLING of the Holy Spirit? How can you actively BE FILLED today?

How is God directing you to POUR FORTH in ministry today? Who has he laid on your heart?

Clearly God is not interested in the most efficient or effective way of accomplishing his work in this world. Did you ever stop to think of that? What he is profoundly interested in is *you*. And me. And the billions of people who inhabit this earth. He is profoundly interested in molding and shaping us—conforming us to the image of his Son. He is profoundly interested in preparing us for the coming kingdom, when we will reign as joint heirs with the Son.

Shadrach, Meshach and Abednego replied to the king, *"O Nebuchadnezzar, we do not need to defend ourselves before you in this matter. If we are thrown into the blazing furnace, the God we serve is able to save us from it, and he will rescue us from your hand, O king. But even if he does not, we want you to know, O king, that we will not serve your gods or worship the image of gold you have set up."*

DANIEL 3:16–18

What is God calling you to ACCEPT today?

What is God calling you to be EMPTIED of, in order to make room for him? Is it something painful from your past, your agenda for today, or something you dream of for tomorrow?

What do you need to be CLEANSED of today? Reflect and confess any known sin; ask God to reveal any areas that need cleansing.

How is your life demonstrating the FILLING of the Holy Spirit? How can you actively BE FILLED today?

How is God directing you to POUR FORTH in ministry today? Who has he laid on your heart?

God is able to deliver us from any circumstance. If he allows us to remain in a trial, it's because he wants us to learn from it.

O Jerusalem, Jerusalem, you who kill the prophets and stone those sent to you, how often I have longed to gather your children together, as a hen gathers her chicks under her wings, but you were not willing.
MATTHEW 23:37

What is God calling you to ACCEPT today?

What is God calling you to be EMPTIED of, in order to make room for him? Is it something painful from your past, your agenda for today, or something you dream of for tomorrow?

What do you need to be CLEANSED of today? Reflect and confess any known sin; ask God to reveal any areas that need cleansing.

How is your life demonstrating the FILLING of the Holy Spirit?
How can you actively BE FILLED today?

How is God directing you to POUR FORTH in ministry today?
Who has he laid on your heart?

Yes, it is God who longs for us, but we are not willing. We
are not willing to take the time to get to know him. Not willing to invest time in his Word. Not willing to talk with him
in prayer. Not willing to walk with him in daily obedience.
Have you ever stopped to consider how much your indiffer-
ence grieves the heart of God? Allow God the joy of
gathering you under his wings.

How great is the love the Father has lavished on us that we should be called children of God! And that is what we are!
1 JOHN 3:1

What is God calling you to ACCEPT today?

What is God calling you to be EMPTIED of, in order to make room for him? Is it something painful from your past, your agenda for today, or something you dream of for tomorrow?

What do you need to be CLEANSED of today? Reflect and confess any known sin; ask God to reveal any areas that need cleansing.

How is your life demonstrating the FILLING of the Holy Spirit? How can you actively BE FILLED today?

How is God directing you to POUR FORTH in ministry today? Who has he laid on your heart?

As long as we come to Scripture out of a sense of duty or as part of a self-improvement program, we're trying to draw water from the desert. It's only as we realize the incredible privilege we have been given—the right to be called children of God—that we can even begin to take joy in his Word.

All Scripture is God-breathed and is useful for teaching, rebuking, correcting and training in righteousness, so that the man of God may be thoroughly equipped for every good work.
2 TIMOTHY 3:16–17

What is God calling you to ACCEPT today?

What is God calling you to be EMPTIED of, in order to make room for him? Is it something painful from your past, your agenda for today, or something you dream of for tomorrow?

What do you need to be CLEANSED of today? Reflect and confess any known sin; ask God to reveal any areas that need cleansing.

How is your life demonstrating the FILLING of the Holy Spirit? How can you actively BE FILLED today?

How is God directing you to POUR FORTH in ministry today? Who has he laid on your heart?

If you want to become a vessel God can use, you must come to know and trust your potter. The place to cultivate that relationship is on your knees and in his Word. At a very minimum, every Christian who has the incredible privilege of owning a copy of the Bible (most people throughout the world and throughout history have not had that privilege) should read through it once a year.

Blessed is the [woman] *who does not walk in the counsel of the wicked or stand in the way of sinners or sit in the seat of mockers. But* [her] *delight is in the law of the Lord, and on his law* [she] *meditates day and night.* [She] *is like a tree planted by streams of water, which yields its fruit in season and whose leaf does not wither. Whatever* [she] *does prospers.*
PSALM 1:1–3

What is God calling you to ACCEPT today?

What is God calling you to be EMPTIED of, in order to make room for him? Is it something painful from your past, your agenda for today, or something you dream of for tomorrow?

What do you need to be CLEANSED of today? Reflect and confess any known sin; ask God to reveal any areas that need cleansing.

How is your life demonstrating the FILLING of the Holy Spirit? How can you actively BE FILLED today?

How is God directing you to POUR FORTH in ministry today? Who has he laid on your heart?

Notice the progression in today's passage. First you're walking by a tempting situation; then it gets your attention, so you stop and stand to take a closer look. Next thing you know, you're sitting down with mockers. Sounds like the lure of TV, doesn't it? You're walking through the family room and a show catches your eye. You stand to watch it for a few minutes, and the next thing you know you're plopped down on the couch. Four hours later, you've got a mind full of mush. Instead, you could have devoted that time to meditating on God's Word!

Oh, how I love your law! I meditate on it all day long. Your commands make me wiser than my enemies, for they are ever with me. I have more insight than all my teachers, for I meditate on your statutes.
PSALM 119:97–99

What is God calling you to ACCEPT today?

What is God calling you to be EMPTIED of, in order to make room for him? Is it something painful from your past, your agenda for today, or something you dream of for tomorrow?

What do you need to be CLEANSED of today? Reflect and confess any known sin; ask God to reveal any areas that need cleansing.

How is your life demonstrating the FILLING of the Holy Spirit?
How can you actively BE FILLED today?

How is God directing you to POUR FORTH in ministry today?
Who has he laid on your heart?

In order to be a useable vessel, you must not only get into
God's Word but it must get into you. Unfortunately, the
New Age gurus and Eastern mystics have given meditation
a bad name. When we think of meditation, we think of chant-
ing "ummmmm" with our legs crossed, trying to drive away
bad Karma. Nevertheless, meditation is an important tool for
molding us into the kind of vessel God can use.

How can a young man keep his way pure? By living *according to your word. I seek you with all my heart; do not let me stray from your commands. I have hidden your word in my heart that I might not sin against you. Praise be to you, O Lord; teach me your decrees. With my lips I recount all the laws that come from your mouth. I rejoice in following your statutes as one rejoices in great riches. I meditate on your precepts and consider your ways. I delight in your decrees; I will not neglect your word.*
PSALM 119: 9–16

What is God calling you to ACCEPT today?

What is God calling you to be EMPTIED of, in order to make room for him? Is it something painful from your past, your agenda for today, or something you dream of for tomorrow?

What do you need to be CLEANSED of today? Reflect and confess any known sin; ask God to reveal any areas that need cleansing.

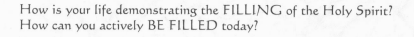

How is your life demonstrating the FILLING of the Holy Spirit? How can you actively BE FILLED today?

How is God directing you to POUR FORTH in ministry today? Who has he laid on your heart?

Before we can meditate on God's Word, we must first hide it in our hearts. A memory bank of Scripture also makes us more spiritually sensitive, which means other women will seek our counsel. Nothing can lift you out of the mire of self-pity faster than helping someone else.

Jesus said to him, "Away from me, Satan! For it is written: 'Worship the Lord your God, and serve him only.'"
MATTHEW 4:10

What is God calling you to ACCEPT today?

What is God calling you to be EMPTIED of, in order to make room for him? Is it something painful from your past, your agenda for today, or something you dream of for tomorrow?

What do you need to be CLEANSED of today? Reflect and confess any known sin; ask God to reveal any areas that need cleansing.

How is your life demonstrating the FILLING of the Holy Spirit?
How can you actively BE FILLED today?

How is God directing you to POUR FORTH in ministry today?
Who has he laid on your heart?

When you know Scripture, you can stand firm in the face of
demonic attacks. When Satan tempted Jesus in the wilder-
ness, he responded with confidence. He knew what God had
said. Remember, Satan is the Father of Lies, and the only
way to cut through his lies is with the Truth. Jesus said,
"You shall know the truth and the truth will set you free."
He also said, "I am the . . . Truth." Know the Word and
know your Lord!

But we have this treasure in jars of clay to show that this
all-surpassing power is from God and not from us.
2 CORINTHIANS 4:7

What is God calling you to ACCEPT today?

What is God calling you to be EMPTIED of, in order to make
room for him? Is it something painful from your past, your agenda
for today, or something you dream of for tomorrow?

What do you need to be CLEANSED of today? Reflect and
confess any known sin; ask God to reveal any areas that need
cleansing.

How is your life demonstrating the FILLING of the Holy Spirit?
How can you actively BE FILLED today?

How is God directing you to POUR FORTH in ministry today?
Who has he laid on your heart?

Did you ever stop to think that God could easily have given us incorruptible bodies and morally flawless character? He could have fashioned us out of a material that would never fade, blemish, or blow it. So why did He make us out of clay? So that it would be absolutely obvious that anything of eternal value accomplished through our lives is from God and not from us. God created us to bring glory to him, not glory to ourselves. God will not share His glory with another.

But who are you, O man, to talk back to God? *"Shall what is formed say to him who formed it, 'Why did you make me like this?'" Does not the potter have the right to make out of the same lump of clay some pottery for noble purposes and some for common use?*
ROMANS 9:20–21

What is God calling you to ACCEPT today?

What is God calling you to be EMPTIED of, in order to make room for him? Is it something painful from your past, your agenda for today, or something you dream of for tomorrow?

What do you need to be CLEANSED of today? Reflect and confess any known sin; ask God to reveal any areas that need cleansing.

How is your life demonstrating the FILLING of the Holy Spirit? How can you actively BE FILLED today?

How is God directing you to POUR FORTH in ministry today? Who has he laid on your heart?

The woman God can use knows where her value comes from. She is precious because of who created her. She is valuable because of the One who dwells within her, not because of the material he used to fashion her or how he chooses to use her.

Now it is God who makes both us and you stand firm in Christ. He anointed us, set his seal of ownership on us, and put his Spirit in our hearts as a deposit, guaranteeing what is to come.
2 CORINTHIANS 1:21–22

What is God calling you to ACCEPT today?

What is God calling you to be EMPTIED of, in order to make room for him? Is it something painful from your past, your agenda for today, or something you dream of for tomorrow?

What do you need to be CLEANSED of today? Reflect and confess any known sin; ask God to reveal any areas that need cleansing.

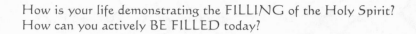

How is your life demonstrating the FILLING of the Holy Spirit?
How can you actively BE FILLED today?

How is God directing you to POUR FORTH in ministry today?
Who has he laid on your heart?

Remember: The world may pass you by, considering you
unremarkable in every way. Yet if you know Jesus Christ, the
God of the Universe dwells within you through the person of
the Holy Spirit. God chose you as his dwelling place and he
desires to work through you.

Each one should test his own actions. Then he can take pride in himself, without comparing himself to somebody else.
GALATIANS 6:4

What is God calling you to ACCEPT today?

What is God calling you to be EMPTIED of, in order to make room for him? Is it something painful from your past, your agenda for today, or something you dream of for tomorrow?

What do you need to be CLEANSED of today? Reflect and confess any known sin; ask God to reveal any areas that need cleansing.

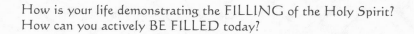

How is your life demonstrating the FILLING of the Holy Spirit? How can you actively BE FILLED today?

How is God directing you to POUR FORTH in ministry today? Who has he laid on your heart?

Have you ever stopped to think that every time you compare yourself to someone else, you are quarreling with your Maker? You are saying, "God, you really messed up this time. You didn't make me the right way. You should have made me like so-and-so." You *are* the vessel God wanted you to be. Accept it and rejoice in your uniqueness, without comparing yourself to anyone else.

For you created my inmost being; you knit me together in my mother's womb. I praise you because I am fearfully and wonderfully made; your works are wonderful, I know that full well. My frame was not hidden from you when I was made in the secret place. When I was woven together in the depths of the earth, your eyes saw my unformed body.

PSALM 139:13–16

What is God calling you to ACCEPT today?

What is God calling you to be EMPTIED of, in order to make room for him? Is it something painful from your past, your agenda for today, or something you dream of for tomorrow?

What do you need to be CLEANSED of today? Reflect and confess any known sin; ask God to reveal any areas that need cleansing.

How is your life demonstrating the FILLING of the Holy Spirit? How can you actively BE FILLED today?

How is God directing you to POUR FORTH in ministry today? Who has he laid on your heart?

God deliberately and carefully created you exactly the way you are. He made you to serve and glorify him in a way that no one else can. He gave you a unique set of talents, physical characteristics, emotional makeup, temperament, and life experiences for a specific reason. Until you fully accept the package God rolled together on the day he created you, you will never become the woman he intended you to be.

Therefore, if anyone is in Christ, he is a new creation; *the old has gone, the new has come! All this is from God, who reconciled us to himself through Christ and gave us the ministry of reconciliation.*
    2 CORINTHIANS 5:17–18

What is God calling you to ACCEPT today?

What is God calling you to be EMPTIED of, in order to make room for him? Is it something painful from your past, your agenda for today, or something you dream of for tomorrow?

What do you need to be CLEANSED of today? Reflect and confess any known sin; ask God to reveal any areas that need cleansing.

How is your life demonstrating the FILLING of the Holy Spirit? How can you actively BE FILLED today?

How is God directing you to POUR FORTH in ministry today? Who has he laid on your heart?

From the moment you encounter Jesus Christ, who you once were no longer matters. It doesn't matter where you've been or what you've done. All that matters is who you are in Him and who you are destined to become. The Bible says if any-one is in Christ, she is a new creation, a person reconciled to God, regardless of past mistakes.

Many of the Samaritans from that town believed in him because of the woman's testimony, "He told me everything I ever did." So when the Samaritans came to him, they urged him to stay with them, and he stayed two days. And because of his words many more became believers. They said to the woman, "We no longer believe just because of what you said; now we have heard for ourselves, and we know that this man really is the Savior of the world."
JOHN 4:39–42

What is God calling you to ACCEPT today?

What is God calling you to be EMPTIED of, in order to make room for him? Is it something painful from your past, your agenda for today, or something you dream of for tomorrow?

What do you need to be CLEANSED of today? Reflect and confess any known sin; ask God to reveal any areas that need cleansing.

How is your life demonstrating the FILLING of the Holy Spirit? How can you actively BE FILLED today?

How is God directing you to POUR FORTH in ministry today? Who has he laid on your heart?

The Samaritan woman didn't have impressive credentials—spiritual, social, or otherwise—but she knew enough to listen to Jesus and to consider his claims upon her life. She didn't pretend to have all the right answers, but she was willing to pose the right questions. And she was willing to point people to Christ so they too could make their own decisions about his claims. No matter who you are or what mistakes you've made, the most important thing you can know about yourself is whether or not you have encountered Christ.

For I resolved to know nothing while I was with you except Jesus Christ and him crucified. I came to you in weakness and fear, and with much trembling. My message and my preaching were not with wise and persuasive words, but with a demonstration of the Spirit's power, so that your faith might not rest on men's wisdom, but on God's power.
1 CORINTHIANS 2:2–5

What is God calling you to ACCEPT today?

What is God calling you to be EMPTIED of, in order to make room for him? Is it something painful from your past, your agenda for today, or something you dream of for tomorrow?

What do you need to be CLEANSED of today? Reflect and confess any known sin; ask God to reveal any areas that need cleansing.

How is your life demonstrating the FILLING of the Holy Spirit? How can you actively BE FILLED today?

How is God directing you to POUR FORTH in ministry today? Who has he laid on your heart?

With each passing day, I become more determined to know nothing except Christ and him crucified. I don't have all the answers. I haven't arrived. I don't have the perfect life. I only know that Jesus Christ has done something incredible in my life. I was lost and now I'm found. I was blind and now I see. I used to be at Point A and now I'm at Point C. Hey, it's not Point Z; it's not Nirvana. But it's forward progress. And the only way I can explain how I got from where I started to where I am now is through God's power.

But the Lord said to Samuel, *"Do not consider his appear-ance or his height, for I have rejected him. The Lord does not look at the things man looks at. Man looks at the outward appearance, but the Lord looks at the heart."*
1 SAMUEL 16:7

What is God calling you to ACCEPT today?

What is God calling you to be EMPTIED of, in order to make room for him? Is it something painful from your past, your agenda for today, or something you dream of for tomorrow?

What do you need to be CLEANSED of today? Reflect and confess any known sin; ask God to reveal any areas that need cleansing.

How is your life demonstrating the FILLING of the Holy Spirit?
How can you actively BE FILLED today?

How is God directing you to POUR FORTH in ministry today?
Who has he laid on your heart?

I may not look perfect on the outside, but I'm changing
inside. Nothing magical, but I've lost a pound of sin here and
an ounce of crummy attitude there. I may not make the cover
of "*Super Christian Today,*" but I'm pressing onward in the
faith. My Creator has done something powerful and
unexplainable in my life and no one can take it away from
me. I blow it every day of my life, but I'm not who I used to
be and I'm not who I would have been.

Do not judge, *or you too will be judged. For in the same way you judge others, you will be judged, and with the measure you use, it will be measured to you.*
MATTHEW 7:1–2

What is God calling you to ACCEPT today?

What is God calling you to be EMPTIED of, in order to make room for him? Is it something painful from your past, your agenda for today, or something you dream of for tomorrow?

What do you need to be CLEANSED of today? Reflect and confess any known sin; ask God to reveal any areas that need cleansing.

How is your life demonstrating the FILLING of the Holy Spirit? How can you actively BE FILLED today?

How is God directing you to POUR FORTH in ministry today? Who has he laid on your heart?

Judging another human being is no business for mere mortals. The truth is you have no idea how far another person has traveled in her spiritual journey. She may be at Point B, but God may have done a mighty work in her life to get her there. She may have experienced heaping doses of the "God Thing." In contrast, a woman who appears to have it all together—a woman at Point Q—may have experienced a very small dose of the God factor, or maybe none at all.

Now if we are children, then we are heirs—heirs of God and co-heirs with Christ.
ROMANS 8:17

What is God calling you to ACCEPT today?

What is God calling you to be EMPTIED of, in order to make room for him? Is it something painful from your past, your agenda for today, or something you dream of for tomorrow?

What do you need to be CLEANSED of today? Reflect and confess any known sin; ask God to reveal any areas that need cleansing.

How is your life demonstrating the FILLING of the Holy Spirit?
How can you actively BE FILLED today?

How is God directing you to POUR FORTH in ministry today?
Who has he laid on your heart?

Let's think about what it means to be heirs of the father:
Since God is the King and we are his daughters (co-heirs
with Jesus, the Prince of Peace), that makes each and every
one of us a princess. Cool! Where's my tiara?

And why do you worry about clothes? See how the lilies of the field grow. They do not labor or spin. Yet I tell you that not even Solomon in all his splendor was dressed like one of these. If that is how God clothes the grass of the field, which is here today and tomorrow is thrown into the fire, will he not much more clothe you, O you of little faith? So do not worry, saying, "What shall we eat?" or "What shall we drink?" or "What shall we wear?" For the pagans run after all these things, and your heavenly Father knows that you need them. But seek first his kingdom and his righteousness, and all these things will be given to you as well. Therefore do not worry about tomorrow, for tomorrow will worry about itself. Each day has enough trouble of its own.
MATTHEW 6:28–34

What is God calling you to ACCEPT today?

What is God calling you to be EMPTIED of, in order to make room for him? Is it something painful from your past, your agenda for today, or something you dream of for tomorrow?

What do you need to be CLEANSED of today? Reflect and confess any known sin; ask God to reveal any areas that need cleansing.

How is your life demonstrating the FILLING of the Holy Spirit? How can you actively BE FILLED today?

How is God directing you to POUR FORTH in ministry today? Who has he laid on your heart?

If we want to be used by God, we've got to make a 180-degree turn. We've got to be emptied of our own private agendas and focus entirely on God's agenda. It's called seeking first the kingdom, and it's a whole lot easier said than done. It means placing your confidence in God and God alone. It requires humbling yourself enough to recognize your total dependence upon God.

Your attitude should be the same as that of Christ *Jesus: Who, being in very nature God, did not consider equality with God something to be grasped, but made himself nothing, taking the very nature of a servant.*
    PHILIPPIANS 2:5–7

What is God calling you to ACCEPT today?

What is God calling you to be EMPTIED of, in order to make room for him? Is it something painful from your past, your agenda for today, or something you dream of for tomorrow?

What do you need to be CLEANSED of today? Reflect and confess any known sin; ask God to reveal any areas that need cleansing.

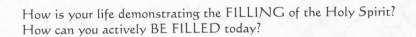

How is your life demonstrating the FILLING of the Holy Spirit? How can you actively BE FILLED today?

How is God directing you to POUR FORTH in ministry today? Who has he laid on your heart?

Just as Christ emptied himself on the cross, so must we be emptied of our private agendas, our hidden longings, our selfish dreams and desires.

And being found in appearance as a man, he humbled him-self and became obedient to death—even death on a cross!
PHILIPPIANS 2:8

What is God calling you to ACCEPT today?

What is God calling you to be EMPTIED of, in order to make room for him? Is it something painful from your past, your agenda for today, or something you dream of for tomorrow?

What do you need to be CLEANSED of today? Reflect and confess any known sin; ask God to reveal any areas that need cleansing.

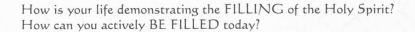

How is your life demonstrating the FILLING of the Holy Spirit? How can you actively BE FILLED today?

How is God directing you to POUR FORTH in ministry today? Who has he laid on your heart?

Even during his torturous death, Jesus wasn't looking out for himself; he was looking out for us. In short, he emptied himself. If we want to become vessels God can use, the very first step is to be emptied. It's really basic when you think about it: There is simply no room for God to work in a life that's already full of itself. There's no room for the blessings he wants to pour into us.

Going a little farther, he fell with his face to the ground and prayed, "My Father, if it is possible, may this cup be taken from me. Yet not as I will, but as you will."
MATTHEW 26:39

What is God calling you to ACCEPT today?

What is God calling you to be EMPTIED of, in order to make room for him? Is it something painful from your past, your agenda for today, or something you dream of for tomorrow?

What do you need to be CLEANSED of today? Reflect and confess any known sin; ask God to reveal any areas that need cleansing.

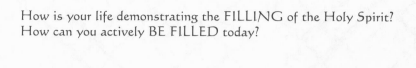

How is your life demonstrating the FILLING of the Holy Spirit?
How can you actively BE FILLED today?

How is God directing you to POUR FORTH in ministry today?
Who has he laid on your heart?

Stay focused on God and his agenda, rather than yourself
and your own convenience. If Christ were interested in his
own comfort, or the convenience of life's here-and-now, he
never would have gone to the cross. Recall Jesus' plea in the
Garden of Gethsemane: He went to the cross because he
stayed focused on God's eternal agenda.

Do everything without complaining or arguing, so that you may become blameless and pure, children of God without fault in a crooked and depraved generation, in which you shine like stars in the universe.
PHILIPPIANS 2:14–15

What is God calling you to ACCEPT today?

What is God calling you to be EMPTIED of, in order to make room for him? Is it something painful from your past, your agenda for today, or something you dream of for tomorrow?

What do you need to be CLEANSED of today? Reflect and confess any known sin; ask God to reveal any areas that need cleansing.

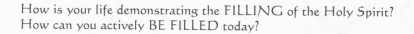

How is your life demonstrating the FILLING of the Holy Spirit?
How can you actively BE FILLED today?

How is God directing you to POUR FORTH in ministry today?
Who has he laid on your heart?

If you really want to be emptied of yourself, so you can enjoy
maximum effectiveness in ministry, there's no more vital step
than actively cultivating a thankful heart. Rather than
demanding more from God, realize that you don't deserve
even one of the blessings he has already given you. Why not
make a list of everything you have to be thankful for?

There is only one Lawgiver and Judge, the one who is able to save and destroy. But you—who are you to judge your neighbor?
JAMES 4:12

What is God calling you to ACCEPT today?

What is God calling you to be EMPTIED of, in order to make room for him? Is it something painful from your past, your agenda for today, or something you dream of for tomorrow?

What do you need to be CLEANSED of today? Reflect and confess any known sin; ask God to reveal any areas that need cleansing.

How is your life demonstrating the FILLING of the Holy Spirit? How can you actively BE FILLED today?

How is God directing you to POUR FORTH in ministry today? Who has he laid on your heart?

Too often, rather than loving and serving people—treating them the way we would want to be treated—we pass judgment. We criticize and condemn. God can't use a woman with a critical spirit! We've got to be humble enough—we've got to be so emptied of ourselves—that we can admit we don't know the full story. We can't possibly know all that a person has gone through or how far they've come. Why not? *Because we're not God.* We may act like we think we're God, but we're not God.

Do you think I cannot call on my Father, and he will at once put at my disposal more than twelve legions of angels? But how then would the Scriptures be fulfilled that say it must happen in this way?
MATTHEW 26:53–54

What is God calling you to ACCEPT today?

What is God calling you to be EMPTIED of, in order to make room for him? Is it something painful from your past, your agenda for today, or something you dream of for tomorrow?

What do you need to be CLEANSED of today? Reflect and confess any known sin; ask God to reveal any areas that need cleansing.

How is your life demonstrating the FILLING of the Holy Spirit? How can you actively BE FILLED today?

How is God directing you to POUR FORTH in ministry today? Who has he laid on your heart?

Jesus easily could have used his influence in the heavenlies to get out of going to the cross. However, Jesus wasn't about the business of using God for his own convenience. Instead, he was willing to be used by God to fulfill the Scriptures. If we would become vessels God can use, we must earnestly desire to be used by God, rather than to use God.

But whatever was to my profit I now consider loss for the sake of Christ. What is more, I consider everything a loss compared to the surpassing greatness of knowing Christ Jesus my Lord, for whose sake I have lost all things. I consider them rubbish, that I may gain Christ and be found in him, not having a righteousness of my own that comes from the law, but that which is through faith in Christ—the righteousness that comes from God and is by faith. I want to know Christ and the power of his resurrection and the fellowship of sharing in his sufferings, becoming like him in his death, and so, somehow, to attain to the resurrection from the dead.
PHILIPPIANS 3:7–11

What is God calling you to ACCEPT today?

What is God calling you to be EMPTIED of, in order to make room for him? Is it something painful from your past, your agenda for today, or something you dream of for tomorrow?

What do you need to be CLEANSED of today? Reflect and confess any known sin; ask God to reveal any areas that need cleansing.

How is your life demonstrating the FILLING of the Holy Spirit? How can you actively BE FILLED today?

How is God directing you to POUR FORTH in ministry today? Who has he laid on your heart?

Christ is our greatest example of what it means to be emptied of self, but he is not the only example the Scriptures provide. The apostle Paul also spoke of emptying himself—of throwing away everything he thought he had to offer God. And admitting instead that all his accomplishments, all his zeal, and all his knowledge were just a collection of rubbish compared to what Christ had done. Do you harbor the idea that you can cling to your worldly credentials and still follow Christ? You must be emptied, even of your greatest accomplishments.

Though I myself have reasons for such confidence. If anyone else thinks he has reasons to put confidence in the flesh, I have more: circumcised on the eighth day, of the people of Israel, of the tribe of Benjamin, a Hebrew of Hebrews; in regard to the law, a Pharisee; as for zeal, persecuting the church; as for legalistic righteousness, faultless.

PHILIPPIANS 3:4–6

What is God calling you to ACCEPT today?

What is God calling you to be EMPTIED of, in order to make room for him? Is it something painful from your past, your agenda for today, or something you dream of for tomorrow?

What do you need to be CLEANSED of today? Reflect and confess any known sin; ask God to reveal any areas that need cleansing.

How is your life demonstrating the FILLING of the Holy Spirit? How can you actively BE FILLED today?

How is God directing you to POUR FORTH in ministry today? Who has he laid on your heart?

Although I didn't start out in life with lots of advantages, I have managed to accomplish a thing or two according to the world's standards. And I struggle to call those accomplishments rubbish. If you're in the same boat, there's only one explanation. You're still full of yourself. You haven't truly been emptied of self. And as long as self remains, Christ doesn't have all the room in your life that he desires. He doesn't have enough room to fully transform you into a vessel he can use.

Not that I have already obtained all this, or have already been made perfect, but I press on to take hold of that for which Christ Jesus took hold of me. Brothers, I do not consider myself yet to have taken hold of it. But one thing I do: Forgetting what is behind and straining toward what is ahead, I press on toward the goal to win the prize for which God has called me heavenward in Christ Jesus.

PHILIPPIANS 3:12–14

What is God calling you to ACCEPT today?

What is God calling you to be EMPTIED of, in order to make room for him? Is it something painful from your past, your agenda for today, or something you dream of for tomorrow?

What do you need to be CLEANSED of today? Reflect and confess any known sin; ask God to reveal any areas that need cleansing.

How is your life demonstrating the FILLING of the Holy Spirit? How can you actively BE FILLED today?

How is God directing you to POUR FORTH in ministry today? Who has he laid on your heart?

A vessel God can use has let go of the pain of the past. We don't let go of the lessons we learned; we don't let go of the ministry opportunities our pain opens up for us; but we do close the wound and let it heal. We don't keep "picking off the scab." Take it from someone who spent many years pickin' scabs—it never brings healing, it only causes more pain.

Do you not know that in a race all the runners run, but only one gets the prize? Run in such a way as to get the prize.
1 CORINTHIANS 9:24

What is God calling you to ACCEPT today?

What is God calling you to be EMPTIED of, in order to make room for him? Is it something painful from your past, your agenda for today, or something you dream of for tomorrow?

What do you need to be CLEANSED of today? Reflect and confess any known sin; ask God to reveal any areas that need cleansing.

How is your life demonstrating the FILLING of the Holy Spirit? How can you actively BE FILLED today?

How is God directing you to POUR FORTH in ministry today? Who has he laid on your heart?

So how do we neutralize the power of the past? How can we be so completely emptied of the past that it can't control us anymore? There's only one way: Jesus Christ. Tony Campolo says, "Your past is an excuse for present behavior until the day you receive Christ." Stop looking back. Stop looking for explanations. Look to the Potter and be emptied of the past. If you do, he will absolutely astound a watching world with what he can accomplish through your life.

All this is from God, who reconciled us to himself through Christ and gave us the ministry of reconciliation: that God was reconciling the world to himself in Christ, not counting men's sins against them. And he has committed to us the message of reconciliation.
2 CORINTHIANS 5:18–19

What is God calling you to ACCEPT today?

What is God calling you to be EMPTIED of, in order to make room for him? Is it something painful from your past, your agenda for today, or something you dream of for tomorrow?

What do you need to be CLEANSED of today? Reflect and confess any known sin; ask God to reveal any areas that need cleansing.

How is your life demonstrating the FILLING of the Holy Spirit?
How can you actively BE FILLED today?

How is God directing you to POUR FORTH in ministry today?
Who has he laid on your heart?

No doubt God has allowed you to endure painful trials in
your life. The only question is: What will you do with that
pain? Will you allow it to cleanse you and transform you into
a vessel God can use to minister to a hurting world? Or will
you let it make you bitter? God wants to use your past to
affect other people's futures, but the choice is entirely yours.
You can be a minister of reconciliation, if only you are willing.

Praise be to the God and Father of our Lord Jesus Christ, the Father of compassion and the God of all comfort, who comforts us in all our troubles, so that we can comfort those in any trouble with the comfort we ourselves have received from God. For just as the sufferings of Christ flow over into our lives, so also through Christ our comfort overflows.

2 CORINTHIANS 1:3–5

What is God calling you to ACCEPT today?

What is God calling you to be EMPTIED of, in order to make room for him? Is it something painful from your past, your agenda for today, or something you dream of for tomorrow?

What do you need to be CLEANSED of today? Reflect and confess any known sin; ask God to reveal any areas that need cleansing.

How is your life demonstrating the FILLING of the Holy Spirit? How can you actively BE FILLED today?

How is God directing you to POUR FORTH in ministry today? Who has he laid on your heart?

Even those of us who've followed Christ for many years through hard, hard places are amazed to discover pockets of resistance in our hearts. Places where we continue to hold out for what we want, regardless of what God wants. As God takes you through your own emptying process, I trust you will find the same comfort I have been comforted with: the knowledge that every road we go down, God goes down before us. And every step we take has been appointed from the beginning, either to help us grow or to help us point the way for others.

If we claim to be without sin, we deceive ourselves and the truth is not in us. If we confess our sins, he is faithful and just and will forgive us our sins and purify us from all unrighteousness.
1 JOHN 1:8–9

What is God calling you to ACCEPT today?

What is God calling you to be EMPTIED of, in order to make room for him? Is it something painful from your past, your agenda for today, or something you dream of for tomorrow?

What do you need to be CLEANSED of today? Reflect and confess any known sin; ask God to reveal any areas that need cleansing.

How is your life demonstrating the FILLING of the Holy Spirit? How can you actively BE FILLED today?

How is God directing you to POUR FORTH in ministry today? Who has he laid on your heart?

Nowhere in Scripture does God promise to cleanse us of unconfessed sin. Unfortunately, sin sometimes has a way of sneaking up on us. We wake up one day and realize we've been wallowing in unconfessed sin for months. Usually, the wake-up call comes in the form of reaping consequences. If we're fortunate enough to have the right people in our lives, the wake-up call can be delivered by a trusted friend. A friend who loves you enough to tell you the truth about your spiritual condition is one of the greatest gifts God gives.

I wait for the Lord, my soul waits, and in his word I put my hope. My soul waits for the Lord more than watchmen wait for the morning, more than watchmen wait for the morning.
PSALM 130: 5–6

What is God calling you to ACCEPT today?

What is God calling you to be EMPTIED of, in order to make room for him? Is it something painful from your past, your agenda for today, or something you dream of for tomorrow?

What do you need to be CLEANSED of today? Reflect and confess any known sin; ask God to reveal any areas that need cleansing.

How is your life demonstrating the FILLING of the Holy Spirit? How can you actively BE FILLED today?

How is God directing you to POUR FORTH in ministry today? Who has he laid on your heart?

The greatest lack in Christianity today is that we do not know God. The answer to every complaint of weakness and failure, the message to every congregation or convention seeking instruction on holiness, should simply be: Where is your God? If you really believe in God, he will put it all right. God is willing and able by his Holy Spirit. Stop expecting the solution from yourself, or the answer from anything there is in man, and simply yield yourself completely to God to work in you. . . . Pray to God that we might get some right conception of what influence could be made by a life spent not in thought or imagination or effort, but in the power of the Holy Spirit, wholly waiting upon God.

—*Waiting on God,* Andrew Murray

"Woe to me!" I cried. *"I am ruined! For I am a man of unclean lips, and I live among a people of unclean lips, and my eyes have seen the King, the Lord Almighty."*
ISAIAH 6:5

What is God calling you to ACCEPT today?

What is God calling you to be EMPTIED of, in order to make room for him? Is it something painful from your past, your agenda for today, or something you dream of for tomorrow?

What do you need to be CLEANSED of today? Reflect and confess any known sin; ask God to reveal any areas that need cleansing.

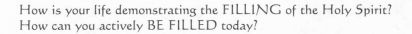

How is your life demonstrating the FILLING of the Holy Spirit? How can you actively BE FILLED today?

How is God directing you to POUR FORTH in ministry today? Who has he laid on your heart?

The more we see God for who he is—the more we behold his holiness—the more we will see our need of cleansing. It is inevitable. If we were to encounter God as Isaiah did, we would have the same reaction. When you meet with God in prayer and he continues to reveal more of himself to you, holiness will be the natural outgrowth.

Have mercy on me, O God, *according to your unfailing love; according to your great compassion blot out my transgressions. Wash away all my iniquity and cleanse me from my sin. For I know my transgressions, and my sin is always before me.*
Against you, you only, have I sinned and done what is evil in your sight, so that you are proved right when you speak and justified when you judge. Surely I was sinful at birth, sinful from the time my mother conceived me. Surely you desire truth in the inner parts; you teach me wisdom in the inmost place. Cleanse me with hyssop, and I will be clean; wash me, and I will be whiter than snow.
PSALM 51:1–7

What is God calling you to ACCEPT today?

What is God calling you to be EMPTIED of, in order to make room for him? Is it something painful from your past, your agenda for today, or something you dream of for tomorrow?

What do you need to be CLEANSED of today? Reflect and confess any known sin; ask God to reveal any areas that need cleansing.

How is your life demonstrating the FILLING of the Holy Spirit?
How can you actively BE FILLED today?

How is God directing you to POUR FORTH in ministry today?
Who has he laid on your heart?

Here's a test you can take to see whether or not you are
allowing the Holy Spirit to do his work of cleansing in your
life: What specific sin did the Holy Spirit convict you of this
past week? What specific thing did you do or say—or fail to
do or say—that the Holy Spirit revealed you needed to
repent of? I would like to suggest to you that if you don't
have an answer it isn't because you didn't sin. It's because
you are not allowing the Holy Spirit the time he needs to
convict and to cleanse you of sin.

Consider it pure joy, my [sisters], *whenever you face trials of many kinds, because you know that the testing of your faith develops perseverance. Perseverance must finish its work so that you may be mature and complete, not lacking anything.*
JAMES 1:2–4

What is God calling you to ACCEPT today?

What is God calling you to be EMPTIED of, in order to make room for him? Is it something painful from your past, your agenda for today, or something you dream of for tomorrow?

What do you need to be CLEANSED of today? Reflect and confess any known sin; ask God to reveal any areas that need cleansing.

How is your life demonstrating the FILLING of the Holy Spirit?
How can you actively BE FILLED today?

How is God directing you to POUR FORTH in ministry today?
Who has he laid on your heart?

You have led the perfect life—for you. God has given you
exactly, precisely, perfectly, the life experiences you need to
become a vessel he can use. God does not delight in your
foibles and failures, but in his mercy he redeems them, using
them to move you forward in the journey. As a vessel hand-
made by God and chosen for his service, you can be confident
that he will use every circumstance—even those you "bring
upon yourself"—to bring you closer to complete maturity.

And we know that in all things God works for the good of those who love him, who have been called according to his purpose.
ROMANS 8:28

What is God calling you to ACCEPT today?

What is God calling you to be EMPTIED of, in order to make room for him? Is it something painful from your past, your agenda for today, or something you dream of for tomorrow?

What do you need to be CLEANSED of today? Reflect and confess any known sin; ask God to reveal any areas that need cleansing.

How is your life demonstrating the FILLING of the Holy Spirit? How can you actively BE FILLED today?

How is God directing you to POUR FORTH in ministry today? Who has he laid on your heart?

When tragedy strikes, the only way we can survive with our sanity and our faith intact is to refuse to demand an explanation from God. The moment we start functioning in the realm of "why," we're in the danger zone. The only safe and sane questions to ask are: "What now, Lord?" "Where do you want me to go from here?" and "How can I take this pain and use it to minister to others?" God is in the redemption business. When we turn our pain over to him, he redeems it and turns it into something good.

Create in me a pure heart, O God, and renew a steadfast spirit within me. Do not cast me from your presence or take your Holy Spirit from me. Restore to me the joy of your salvation and grant me a willing spirit, to sustain me. Then I will teach transgressors your ways, and sinners will turn back to you.
PSALM 51:10–13

What is God calling you to ACCEPT today?

What is God calling you to be EMPTIED of, in order to make room for him? Is it something painful from your past, your agenda for today, or something you dream of for tomorrow?

What do you need to be CLEANSED of today? Reflect and confess any known sin; ask God to reveal any areas that need cleansing.

How is your life demonstrating the FILLING of the Holy Spirit? How can you actively BE FILLED today?

How is God directing you to POUR FORTH in ministry today? Who has he laid on your heart?

The only way suffering can cleanse rather than destroy us is if we yield our dreams and agendas to his will. God has an eternal plan that our finite minds couldn't possibly conceive. We can't know all the answers. But we can make a decision. Ask yourself now: "Am I willing to allow God to mold me and shape me—using whatever tools, whatever circumstances he chooses?" If you can answer yes, then you can become a vessel God can use.

If we confess our sins, he is faithful and just and will forgive
us our sins and purify us from all unrighteousness.
1 JOHN 1:9

What is God calling you to ACCEPT today?

What is God calling you to be EMPTIED of, in order to make
room for him? Is it something painful from your past, your agenda
for today, or something you dream of for tomorrow?

What do you need to be CLEANSED of today? Reflect and
confess any known sin; ask God to reveal any areas that need
cleansing.

How is your life demonstrating the FILLING of the Holy Spirit?
How can you actively BE FILLED today?

How is God directing you to POUR FORTH in ministry today?
Who has he laid on your heart?

Keep silent and listen to your heart. Hear what it is saying
to you about who you really are and what you really desire.
Turn off the noise and discover what is going on inside you.
Then, once you have confronted the truth, confess your sins
so that God can cleanse you. But as long as you are denying
that you've got a dirty heart, God cannot begin the work of
cleansing.

The Lord is in *his holy temple; let all the earth be silent before him.*
HABAKKUK 2:20

What is God calling you to ACCEPT today?

What is God calling you to be EMPTIED of, in order to make room for him? Is it something painful from your past, your agenda for today, or something you dream of for tomorrow?

What do you need to be CLEANSED of today? Reflect and confess any known sin; ask God to reveal any areas that need cleansing.

How is your life demonstrating the FILLING of the Holy Spirit? How can you actively BE FILLED today?

How is God directing you to POUR FORTH in ministry today? Who has he laid on your heart?

Don't be afraid of silence. Don't let the world deafen you to the truth about your heart's condition. If the silence reveals sin in your heart, confess it. Repent of it. Ask God to cleanse you. Silence is your partner in the process of cleansing. If it reveals dirt, it is doing exactly what it is intended to do. If silence reveals sin in your heart, it's doing its job.

Come with me by yourselves to a quiet place and get
some rest.
       MARK 6:31

What is God calling you to ACCEPT today?

What is God calling you to be EMPTIED of, in order to make
room for him? Is it something painful from your past, your agenda
for today, or something you dream of for tomorrow?

What do you need to be CLEANSED of today? Reflect and
confess any known sin; ask God to reveal any areas that need
cleansing.

How is your life demonstrating the FILLING of the Holy Spirit?
How can you actively BE FILLED today?

How is God directing you to POUR FORTH in ministry today?
Who has he laid on your heart?

Are you avoiding silence or are you cultivating it? Jesus
actively pursued it: He often withdrew from the crowds and
encouraged his disciples to do likewise. We too must learn to
be still. Do you feel compelled to surround yourself with
noise? Can you leave the radio off in the car or in the
kitchen? Could you turn off the ubiquitous TV for a day or a
week or a month or forever?

He who has ears, let him hear.
MATTHEW 11:15

What is God calling you to ACCEPT today?

What is God calling you to be EMPTIED of, in order to make room for him? Is it something painful from your past, your agenda for today, or something you dream of for tomorrow?

What do you need to be CLEANSED of today? Reflect and confess any known sin; ask God to reveal any areas that need cleansing.

How is your life demonstrating the FILLING of the Holy Spirit? How can you actively BE FILLED today?

How is God directing you to POUR FORTH in ministry today? Who has he laid on your heart?

God will sovereignly send his people into your life with words to spark your growth, but your responsibility is to be available and willing to hear their words with an open heart.

But the fruit of the Spirit is love, joy, peace, patience, kindness, goodness, faithfulness, gentleness and self-control. Against such things there is no law. Those who belong to Christ Jesus have crucified the sinful nature with its passions and desires. Since we live by the Spirit, let us keep in step with the Spirit.
GALATIANS 5:22–25

What is God calling you to ACCEPT today?

What is God calling you to be EMPTIED of, in order to make room for him? Is it something painful from your past, your agenda for today, or something you dream of for tomorrow?

What do you need to be CLEANSED of today? Reflect and confess any known sin; ask God to reveal any areas that need cleansing.

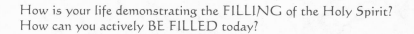

How is your life demonstrating the FILLING of the Holy Spirit?
How can you actively BE FILLED today?

How is God directing you to POUR FORTH in ministry today?
Who has he laid on your heart?

Devoting ourselves to cultivating the spiritual disciplines is
tangible evidence that we are committed to cooperating with
the Holy Spirit in the work of cleansing. As we allow God
to transform us from the inside out, our lives will harvest an
increasing bounty of righteousness—love, joy, peace, patience,
kindness, faithfulness, gentleness, and self-control.

My people have committed two sins: They have forsaken me, the spring of living water, and have dug their own cisterns, broken cisterns that cannot hold water.
JEREMIAH 2:13

What is God calling you to ACCEPT today?

What is God calling you to be EMPTIED of, in order to make room for him? Is it something painful from your past, your agenda for today, or something you dream of for tomorrow?

What do you need to be CLEANSED of today? Reflect and confess any known sin; ask God to reveal any areas that need cleansing.

How is your life demonstrating the FILLING of the Holy Spirit?
How can you actively BE FILLED today?

How is God directing you to POUR FORTH in ministry today?
Who has he laid on your heart?

God created us as empty vessels, designed to be filled only
with him. All of us sense that emptiness inside, and we are
driven to fill it. We can try to fill it with a career, with money,
with a beautifully decorated house, with the right clothes and
makeup and hairstyle. We can try to fill it with food, or
Christian rituals and church busywork. The possibilities are
endless. We need the Living Water that flows from the throne
of God into the lives of those who abide in him. Nothing
less will satisfy.

On the last and greatest day of the Feast, Jesus stood and said in a loud voice, "If anyone is thirsty, let him come to me and drink. Whoever believes in me, as the Scripture has said, streams of living water will flow from within him." By this he meant the Spirit, whom those who believed in him were later to receive.
JOHN 7:37–39

What is God calling you to ACCEPT today?

What is God calling you to be EMPTIED of, in order to make room for him? Is it something painful from your past, your agenda for today, or something you dream of for tomorrow?

What do you need to be CLEANSED of today? Reflect and confess any known sin; ask God to reveal any areas that need cleansing.

How is your life demonstrating the FILLING of the Holy Spirit? How can you actively BE FILLED today?

How is God directing you to POUR FORTH in ministry today? Who has he laid on your heart?

Christ is our very life; there is no life without water. We can only give that which we have received. After all, a vessel cannot create water. It can only pour forth that which is poured into it. In the same way, we must be filled with God's Spirit—filled with the Living Water—if we are to have anything to give others. Being filled with God, with the living water Jesus promised, is not a one-time event. It's a moment-by-moment way of life.

Be filled with the Spirit. *Speak to one another with psalms, hymns and spiritual songs. Sing and make music in your heart to the Lord, always giving thanks to God the Father for everything, in the name of our Lord Jesus Christ.*
EPHESIANS 5:18–20

What is God calling you to ACCEPT today?

What is God calling you to be EMPTIED of, in order to make room for him? Is it something painful from your past, your agenda for today, or something you dream of for tomorrow?

What do you need to be CLEANSED of today? Reflect and confess any known sin; ask God to reveal any areas that need cleansing.

How is your life demonstrating the FILLING of the Holy Spirit?
How can you actively BE FILLED today?

How is God directing you to POUR FORTH in ministry today?
Who has he laid on your heart?

We face two dangers in the church today. The first is this:
water that remains in the vessel too long becomes stagnant.
If all we do is feed our own faith we'll become fat, lazy
Christians. However, the second danger strikes me as even
deadlier. It's giving when you haven't been filled. Take heed:
Before you attempt to pour anything into the precious life of
another human being, make sure you have first been filled.

Jesus replied: *"'Love the Lord your God with all your heart and with all your soul and with all your mind.' This is the first and greatest commandment. And the second is like it: 'Love your neighbor as yourself.'"*
MATTHEW 22:37–39

What is God calling you to ACCEPT today?

What is God calling you to be EMPTIED of, in order to make room for him? Is it something painful from your past, your agenda for today, or something you dream of for tomorrow?

What do you need to be CLEANSED of today? Reflect and confess any known sin; ask God to reveal any areas that need cleansing.

How is your life demonstrating the FILLING of the Holy Spirit? How can you actively BE FILLED today?

How is God directing you to POUR FORTH in ministry today? Who has he laid on your heart?

The degree to which you demonstrate love to family and friends, neighbors, strangers, and even enemies, is an accurate measure of how filled you are with the Holy Spirit.

You have heard that it was said, *"Love your neighbor and hate your enemy." But I tell you: Love your enemies and pray for those who persecute you, that you may be sons of your Father in heaven.*
MATTHEW 5:43–45

What is God calling you to ACCEPT today?

What is God calling you to be EMPTIED of, in order to make room for him? Is it something painful from your past, your agenda for today, or something you dream of for tomorrow?

What do you need to be CLEANSED of today? Reflect and confess any known sin; ask God to reveal any areas that need cleansing.

How is your life demonstrating the FILLING of the Holy Spirit?
How can you actively BE FILLED today?

How is God directing you to POUR FORTH in ministry today?
Who has he laid on your heart?

Do you love your enemies or do you seek revenge? Do you
harbor bitterness against those who have hurt you or are you
quick to forgive? Jesus said we should evaluate our love quo-
tient based on how we treat the people who treat us badly.
God does not get an ounce of glory when we exercise love
when the loving is easy. That's something anyone can do.
But only God can enable us to love those who have hurt us.
And when we do, we get the world's attention. They see
something only God could do, and he gets the glory.

Rejoice in the Lord always. *I will say it again: Rejoice! Let your gentleness be evident to all. The Lord is near. Do not be anxious about anything, but in everything, by prayer and petition, with thanksgiving, present your requests to God. And the peace of God, which transcends all understanding, will guard your hearts and your minds in Christ Jesus.*
PHILIPPIANS 4:4–7

What is God calling you to ACCEPT today?

What is God calling you to be EMPTIED of, in order to make room for him? Is it something painful from your past, your agenda for today, or something you dream of for tomorrow?

What do you need to be CLEANSED of today? Reflect and confess any known sin; ask God to reveal any areas that need cleansing.

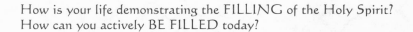

How is your life demonstrating the FILLING of the Holy Spirit?
How can you actively BE FILLED today?

How is God directing you to POUR FORTH in ministry today?
Who has he laid on your heart?

Any run-of-the-mill heathen can rejoice when the good times
roll; what sets us apart—what enables God to bring glory to
himself through our lives—is how we respond when the bad
times come. We rejoice not only for our own sakes but also
for the sake of a watching world. Remember the sole reason
for our existence: to glorify God. If we want to be a vessel
God can use, then choosing to rejoice when everything
around us says "mope and mumble" is an important first step.

Make every effort to live in peace with all men and to be holy; without holiness no one will see the Lord.
HEBREWS 12:14

What is God calling you to ACCEPT today?

What is God calling you to be EMPTIED of, in order to make room for him? Is it something painful from your past, your agenda for today, or something you dream of for tomorrow?

What do you need to be CLEANSED of today? Reflect and confess any known sin; ask God to reveal any areas that need cleansing.

How is your life demonstrating the FILLING of the Holy Spirit? How can you actively BE FILLED today?

How is God directing you to POUR FORTH in ministry today? Who has he laid on your heart?

Do you know what the opposite of a peacemaker is? It's someone who is full of herself. People who want to pursue their agenda, their ideas, and who think they alone have a corner on the truth, are the scourge of every home and church. It goes back to being emptied of self. Until we are emptied, we can't be a channel of peace.

If it is possible, as far as it depends on you, live at peace
with everyone.
      ROMANS 12:18

What is God calling you to ACCEPT today?

What is God calling you to be EMPTIED of, in order to make
room for him? Is it something painful from your past, your agenda
for today, or something you dream of for tomorrow?

What do you need to be CLEANSED of today? Reflect and
confess any known sin; ask God to reveal any areas that need
cleansing.

How is your life demonstrating the FILLING of the Holy Spirit?
How can you actively BE FILLED today?

How is God directing you to POUR FORTH in ministry today?
Who has he laid on your heart?

Unforgiving people are also impatient people, because their
emotional storehouse is always on the verge of overflowing. If
you are impatient, examine your heart and you will discover
that your real problem may be an unforgiving heart. Clinging
to old hurts will not benefit you in any way. It will, however,
prevent you from becoming the useful overflowing vessel God
designed you to be.

A man's wisdom *gives him patience; it is to his glory to* *overlook an offense.*
PROVERBS 19:11

What is God calling you to ACCEPT today?

What is God calling you to be EMPTIED of, in order to make room for him? Is it something painful from your past, your agenda for today, or something you dream of for tomorrow?

What do you need to be CLEANSED of today? Reflect and confess any known sin; ask God to reveal any areas that need cleansing.

How is your life demonstrating the FILLING of the Holy Spirit? How can you actively BE FILLED today?

How is God directing you to POUR FORTH in ministry today? Who has he laid on your heart?

When we are patient with others, we can forgive and overlook offenses. And when we forgive, we'll find we have an entire storehouse filled with patience.

For this very reason, make every effort to add to your faith goodness; and to goodness, knowledge; and to knowledge, self-control; and to self-control, perseverance; and to perseverance, godliness; and to godliness, brotherly kindness; and to brotherly kindness, love. For if you possess these qualities in increasing measure, they will keep you from being ineffective and unproductive in your knowledge of our Lord Jesus Christ.
       2 PETER 1:5–8

What is God calling you to ACCEPT today?

What is God calling you to be EMPTIED of, in order to make room for him? Is it something painful from your past, your agenda for today, or something you dream of for tomorrow?

What do you need to be CLEANSED of today? Reflect and confess any known sin; ask God to reveal any areas that need cleansing.

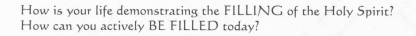

How is your life demonstrating the FILLING of the Holy Spirit? How can you actively BE FILLED today?

How is God directing you to POUR FORTH in ministry today? Who has he laid on your heart?

It is possible to have knowledge of the Lord Jesus Christ and still be ineffective and unproductive. Isn't that a sobering thought? The Bible doesn't guarantee that all of us will be used to further his kingdom. God can use women like us, but we will have to make every effort to add to our faith kindness and goodness.

Terah took his son Abram, *his grandson Lot son of Haran,
and his daughter-in-law Sarai, the wife of his son Abram, and
together they set out from Ur of the Chaldeans to go to Canaan.*
GENESIS 11:31

What is God calling you to ACCEPT today?

What is God calling you to be EMPTIED of, in order to make
room for him? Is it something painful from your past, your agenda
for today, or something you dream of for tomorrow?

What do you need to be CLEANSED of today? Reflect and
confess any known sin; ask God to reveal any areas that need
cleansing.

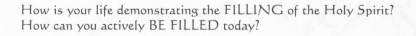

How is your life demonstrating the FILLING of the Holy Spirit? How can you actively BE FILLED today?

How is God directing you to POUR FORTH in ministry today? Who has he laid on your heart?

You can't stay where you are and go with God. Abraham left Ur of the Chaldeans. Moses had to leave Egypt, tend sheep for forty years, return to Egypt, and leave again with God's people. David had to leave tending sheep to do battle with Goliath, and later to become King of Israel. It's a pattern throughout Scripture. What is God calling you to leave behind?

So Abram left, as the Lord had told him.
GENESIS 12:4

What is God calling you to ACCEPT today?

What is God calling you to be EMPTIED of, in order to make room for him? Is it something painful from your past, your agenda for today, or something you dream of for tomorrow?

What do you need to be CLEANSED of today? Reflect and confess any known sin; ask God to reveal any areas that need cleansing.

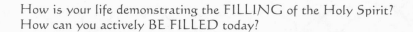

How is your life demonstrating the FILLING of the Holy Spirit? How can you actively BE FILLED today?

How is God directing you to POUR FORTH in ministry today? Who has he laid on your heart?

God accepts us where we are, but he wants us to continue on. Not only for the sake of his kingdom, not only so that we can be vessels fit for his use, but also for our own sake. This is because he made us and he knows how we're wired. He knows that life will be better for us if we make every effort to be filled with kindness and goodness. He knows that only then can we fulfill the very purpose for which we were created: to be a vessel reflecting the glory of God.

Let love and faithfulness never leave you; bind them around your neck, write them on the tablet of your heart. Then you will win favor and a good name in the sight of God and man.
PROVERBS 3:3–4

What is God calling you to ACCEPT today?

What is God calling you to be EMPTIED of, in order to make room for him? Is it something painful from your past, your agenda for today, or something you dream of for tomorrow?

What do you need to be CLEANSED of today? Reflect and confess any known sin; ask God to reveal any areas that need cleansing.

How is your life demonstrating the FILLING of the Holy Spirit? How can you actively BE FILLED today?

How is God directing you to POUR FORTH in ministry today? Who has he laid on your heart?

According to *Strong's Exhaustive Concordance,* a faithful person is stable, trustworthy, established, certain, and true. To be faithful means you know exactly what you believe and you stand by it.

How long will you waver between two opinions? If the Lord is God, follow him.
1 KINGS 18:21

What is God calling you to ACCEPT today?

What is God calling you to be EMPTIED of, in order to make room for him? Is it something painful from your past, your agenda for today, or something you dream of for tomorrow?

What do you need to be CLEANSED of today? Reflect and confess any known sin; ask God to reveal any areas that need cleansing.

How is your life demonstrating the FILLING of the Holy Spirit?
How can you actively BE FILLED today?

How is God directing you to POUR FORTH in ministry today?
Who has he laid on your heart?

Do you waver between two opinions? Maybe in your mind
you are convinced that your life must be filled with Christ;
that your agenda must make way for his. How about the way
you live your daily life? Do you always live as if you believe
your highest calling is to present yourself as an empty vessel,
waiting to be filled with the things of God? If you're like me,
on many, many days you are far too filled with yourself—your
own plans and agenda—to have even the tiniest place for
God. The truth is, God doesn't inhabit tiny places. He is
either Lord of all or he is not Lord at all.

Let your gentleness be evident to all.
PHILIPPIANS 4:5

What is God calling you to ACCEPT today?

What is God calling you to be EMPTIED of, in order to make room for him? Is it something painful from your past, your agenda for today, or something you dream of for tomorrow?

What do you need to be CLEANSED of today? Reflect and confess any known sin; ask God to reveal any areas that need cleansing.

How is your life demonstrating the FILLING of the Holy Spirit? How can you actively BE FILLED today?

How is God directing you to POUR FORTH in ministry today? Who has he laid on your heart?

Gentleness is the outward expression of an inward reality: a heart that is humbled and a life that is emptied of self and yielded to God.

The fruit of the Spirit is ... self-control.
GALATIANS 5:22–23

What is God calling you to ACCEPT today?

What is God calling you to be EMPTIED of, in order to make room for him? Is it something painful from your past, your agenda for today, or something you dream of for tomorrow?

What do you need to be CLEANSED of today? Reflect and confess any known sin; ask God to reveal any areas that need cleansing.

How is your life demonstrating the FILLING of the Holy Spirit? How can you actively BE FILLED today?

How is God directing you to POUR FORTH in ministry today? Who has he laid on your heart?

Outward attempts at self-control won't yield long-term results. You've got to change from the inside out. Don't look to yourself or to a program; look to God. Self-control is a fruit of the Holy Spirit. As you are increasingly filled with the Holy Spirit, you will be filled to increasing measure with self-control. I don't know about you, but I say, "Fill 'er up!"

If anyone hears my voice and opens the door, I will come in and eat with him, and he with me.
REVELATION 3:20

What is God calling you to ACCEPT today?

What is God calling you to be EMPTIED of, in order to make room for him? Is it something painful from your past, your agenda for today, or something you dream of for tomorrow?

What do you need to be CLEANSED of today? Reflect and confess any known sin; ask God to reveal any areas that need cleansing.

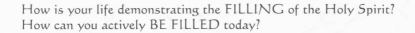

How is your life demonstrating the FILLING of the Holy Spirit? How can you actively BE FILLED today?

How is God directing you to POUR FORTH in ministry today? Who has he laid on your heart?

God has always spoken to his people. God still speaks to his people. If you can't hear God speaking to you, you've got a fundamental problem at the very heart of your Christian life. If you can't hear God speaking, the problem isn't with God, the problem is with you. Rest assured, God wants to communicate with you. He longs for you to hear his voice and to walk in close fellowship with him.

Be joyful always; *pray continually; give thanks in all circumstances, for this is God's will for you in Christ Jesus.*
1 THESSALONIANS 5:16–18

What is God calling you to ACCEPT today?

What is God calling you to be EMPTIED of, in order to make room for him? Is it something painful from your past, your agenda for today, or something you dream of for tomorrow?

What do you need to be CLEANSED of today? Reflect and confess any known sin; ask God to reveal any areas that need cleansing.

How is your life demonstrating the FILLING of the Holy Spirit? How can you actively BE FILLED today?

How is God directing you to POUR FORTH in ministry today? Who has he laid on your heart?

I believe writing out your prayers, or journaling, is one of the most effective ways that we can hear God speaking. As we put pen to paper, ideas spring from deep within our hearts. We open ourselves up in a way we're often afraid to when speaking. And writing forces us to stay focused rather than allowing our minds to drift off. Try writing out your prayers for a week and see the difference it can make.

Call to me and I will answer you and tell you great and *unsearchable things you do not know.*
JEREMIAH 33:3

What is God calling you to ACCEPT today?

What is God calling you to be EMPTIED of, in order to make room for him? Is it something painful from your past, your agenda for today, or something you dream of for tomorrow?

What do you need to be CLEANSED of today? Reflect and confess any known sin; ask God to reveal any areas that need cleansing.

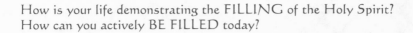

How is your life demonstrating the FILLING of the Holy Spirit?
How can you actively BE FILLED today?

How is God directing you to POUR FORTH in ministry today?
Who has he laid on your heart?

We tend to think God is in the business of keeping secrets,
as if he is sitting on his heavenly throne with his arms
crossed, saying, "You guys figure it out for yourselves."
Nothing could be further from the truth. Have you stopped
to consider how many miracles God performed to prepare and
preserve his Word for us? Read the Word and watch as God
unlocks the secret things before your eyes.

Balaam was riding on his donkey, and his two servants were with him. When the donkey saw the angel of the Lord standing in the road with a drawn sword in his hand, she turned off the road into a field. Balaam beat her to get her back on the road.
NUMBERS 22:22–23

What is God calling you to ACCEPT today?

What is God calling you to be EMPTIED of, in order to make room for him? Is it something painful from your past, your agenda for today, or something you dream of for tomorrow?

What do you need to be CLEANSED of today? Reflect and confess any known sin; ask God to reveal any areas that need cleansing.

How is your life demonstrating the FILLING of the Holy Spirit?
How can you actively BE FILLED today?

How is God directing you to POUR FORTH in ministry today?
Who has he laid on your heart?

When we encounter obstacles, we tend to strike out at whoever or whatever is closest to us. We've got an agenda to
pursue and we resent anything that stands in our way. Here's
an irony worth pondering: We pray for God to remove the
obstacle, when it may very well be that God is the one who
put the obstacle there. The next time you're tempted to pray
that God change your circumstances, stop and think. Maybe
God doesn't want to change the circumstances; he wants to
change you.

Do not be anxious about anything, but in everything, by prayer and petition, with thanksgiving, present your requests to God. And the peace of God, which transcends all understanding, will guard your hearts and your minds in Christ Jesus.
PHILIPPIANS 4:6–7

What is God calling you to ACCEPT today?

What is God calling you to be EMPTIED of, in order to make room for him? Is it something painful from your past, your agenda for today, or something you dream of for tomorrow?

What do you need to be CLEANSED of today? Reflect and confess any known sin; ask God to reveal any areas that need cleansing.

How is your life demonstrating the FILLING of the Holy Spirit? How can you actively BE FILLED today?

How is God directing you to POUR FORTH in ministry today? Who has he laid on your heart?

When life goes awry, that's your clue that God is trying to speak to you. Pay attention! Pray. Study God's Word. Seek counsel from mature Christians. It goes without saying that we don't rely solely on circumstances for guidance. But when we evaluate circumstances in light of what the Holy Spirit is telling us through his Word, through prayer and through fellow believers, we can get a very clear indication of what God is saying.

Teach us to number our days aright, that we may gain a heart of wisdom.
PSALM 90:12

What is God calling you to ACCEPT today?

What is God calling you to be EMPTIED of, in order to make room for him? Is it something painful from your past, your agenda for today, or something you dream of for tomorrow?

What do you need to be CLEANSED of today? Reflect and confess any known sin; ask God to reveal any areas that need cleansing.

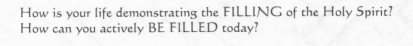

How is your life demonstrating the FILLING of the Holy Spirit? How can you actively BE FILLED today?

How is God directing you to POUR FORTH in ministry today? Who has he laid on your heart?

The fifth and final requirement for becoming a vessel God can use is to pour out your life in ministry as God directs you. Notice that it is not enough to pour your life where you think you are needed; it's not enough to "attempt great things for God" or simply to "find a need and fill it." Your life will be as effective as you are responsive to God's direction.

So God created man in his own image, in the image of God he created him; male and female he created them.
GENESIS 1:27

What is God calling you to ACCEPT today?

What is God calling you to be EMPTIED of, in order to make room for him? Is it something painful from your past, your agenda for today, or something you dream of for tomorrow?

What do you need to be CLEANSED of today? Reflect and confess any known sin; ask God to reveal any areas that need cleansing.

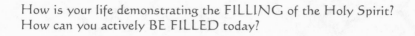

How is your life demonstrating the FILLING of the Holy Spirit? How can you actively BE FILLED today?

How is God directing you to POUR FORTH in ministry today? Who has he laid on your heart?

Just as God by His power once created, so by that same power God must every moment maintain. Man has only to look back to the origin of existence and he will acknowledge that he owes everything to God. Man's chief care, his highest virtue, and his only happiness, now and through all eternity, is to present himself as an empty vessel in which God can dwell and manifest His power and goodness.

—*Humility*, Andrew Murray

What good is it, my brothers, if a man claims to have faith but has no deeds? Can such faith save him? Suppose a brother or sister is without clothes and daily food. If one of you says to him, "Go, I wish you well; keep warm and well fed," but does nothing about his physical needs, what good is it? In the same way, faith by itself, if it is not accompanied by action, is dead. But someone will say, "You have faith; I have deeds." Show me your faith without deeds, and I will show you my faith by what I do.

JAMES 2:14–18

What is God calling you to ACCEPT today?

What is God calling you to be EMPTIED of, in order to make room for him? Is it something painful from your past, your agenda for today, or something you dream of for tomorrow?

What do you need to be CLEANSED of today? Reflect and confess any known sin; ask God to reveal any areas that need cleansing.

How is your life demonstrating the FILLING of the Holy Spirit? How can you actively BE FILLED today?

How is God directing you to POUR FORTH in ministry today? Who has he laid on your heart?

When God shows you what he wants you to do, get involved immediately. Sometimes God will give you a preview of things to come, and what he wants you to do now is to prepare, adjust, and train. You may have to wait days, weeks, even years for the instruction to "Go." When God does give the go-ahead, he will also give you the wisdom and the strength to accomplish his purposes in his timing. You'll get more done in one month of flowing where God directs than you will in a lifetime of doing your own thing for God.

Jesus called them together and said, "You know that those who are regarded as rulers of the Gentiles lord it over them, and their high officials exercise authority over them. Not so with you. Instead, whoever wants to become great among you must be your servant, and whoever wants to be first must be slave of all. For even the Son of Man did not come to be served, but to serve, and to give his life as a ransom for many."

MARK 10:42–45

What is God calling you to ACCEPT today?

What is God calling you to be EMPTIED of, in order to make room for him? Is it something painful from your past, your agenda for today, or something you dream of for tomorrow?

What do you need to be CLEANSED of today? Reflect and confess any known sin; ask God to reveal any areas that need cleansing.

How is your life demonstrating the FILLING of the Holy Spirit?
How can you actively BE FILLED today?

How is God directing you to POUR FORTH in ministry today?
Who has he laid on your heart?

If you desire to be a vessel God can use, you've got to come
to grips with this truth. There is nothing else on earth that
can hinder our effectiveness—and prevent us from experiencing joy in our everyday lives—like an attitude that says, "I
have not come to minister but to be ministered unto. I have
not come to serve but to be served." If we expect to sit back
and be served in the kingdom, we have not known or seen
Jesus. Neither have we understood his message.

At that time the disciples came to Jesus and asked, "Who is the greatest in the kingdom of heaven?" He called a little child and had him stand among them. And he said: "I tell you the truth, unless you change and become like little children, you will never enter the kingdom of heaven. Therefore, whoever humbles himself like this child is the greatest in the kingdom of heaven."
MATTHEW 18:1–4

What is God calling you to ACCEPT today?

What is God calling you to be EMPTIED of, in order to make room for him? Is it something painful from your past, your agenda for today, or something you dream of for tomorrow?

What do you need to be CLEANSED of today? Reflect and confess any known sin; ask God to reveal any areas that need cleansing.

How is your life demonstrating the FILLING of the Holy Spirit?
How can you actively BE FILLED today?

How is God directing you to POUR FORTH in ministry today?
Who has he laid on your heart?

Let me give you a little self-test that you can take before
starting any ministry project or doing any good deed. Ask
yourself: Can I do this without expecting anything in return?
If the answer is no, don't do it. Whether you expect a thank-
you note, praise, approval, a plaque, or a wing of the church
named after you, if you expect anything at all—other than to
hear from your Master's lips, "Well done, good and faithful
servant"—don't do it. If you enter into ministry with a secret
desire to be ministered unto rather than to minister, your
efforts will bring you heartache rather than joy.

As the Father has loved me, so have I loved you. Now remain in my love. If you obey my commands, you will remain in my love, just as I have obeyed my Father's commands and remain in his love. I have told you this so that my joy may be in you and that your joy may be complete. My command is this: Love each other as I have loved you. Greater love has no one than this, that one lay down his life for his friends. You are my friends if you do what I command.
JOHN 15:9–14

What is God calling you to ACCEPT today?

What is God calling you to be EMPTIED of, in order to make room for him? Is it something painful from your past, your agenda for today, or something you dream of for tomorrow?

What do you need to be CLEANSED of today? Reflect and confess any known sin; ask God to reveal any areas that need cleansing.

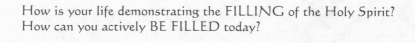

How is your life demonstrating the FILLING of the Holy Spirit? How can you actively BE FILLED today?

How is God directing you to POUR FORTH in ministry today? Who has he laid on your heart?

All performance-based religions are man-made, no matter how great the theological foundation appears. Genuine Christianity is not about performance but about a relationship. It's about the God of the universe reaching down and initiating a personal love relationship with sinful people like you and me. It's all about love.

Let us fix our eyes on Jesus, the author and perfecter of our faith, who for the joy set before him endured the cross, scorning its shame, and sat down at the right hand of the throne of God. Consider him who endured such opposition from sinful men, so that you will not grow weary and lose heart.
HEBREWS 12:2–3

What is God calling you to ACCEPT today?

What is God calling you to be EMPTIED of, in order to make room for him? Is it something painful from your past, your agenda for today, or something you dream of for tomorrow?

What do you need to be CLEANSED of today? Reflect and confess any known sin; ask God to reveal any areas that need cleansing.

How is your life demonstrating the FILLING of the Holy Spirit? How can you actively BE FILLED today?

How is God directing you to POUR FORTH in ministry today? Who has he laid on your heart?

Why did Jesus endure the cross? For the joy set before him. What joy was that? Was it the joy of hearing men's applause? Was it the joy of having "everything turning up roses"? Was it the joy of winning a popularity contest? No. It was the deep and abiding joy that only comes when we allow the Father to accomplish his work through us. It is the joy that can only come when we are truly a vessel God can use. It is the joy that comes when we look only to eternity for our rewards.

Thank you for selecting a book from
BETHANY HOUSE PUBLISHERS

Bethany House Publishers is a ministry of Bethany Fellowship International, an interdenominational, nonprofit organization committed to spreading the Good News of Jesus Christ around the world through evangelism, church planting, literature distribution, and care for those in need. Missionary training is offered through Bethany College of Missions.

Bethany Fellowship International is a member of the National Association of Evangelicals and subscribes to its statement of faith. If you would like further information, please contact:

Bethany Fellowship International
6820 Auto Club Road
Minneapolis, MN 55438 USA

SMITH
WIGGLESWORTH
ON
HEAVEN

Other Whitaker House Titles
by Smith Wigglesworth

Ever Increasing Faith

Experiencing God's Power Today

Greater Works

The Power of Faith

Smith Wigglesworth Devotional

Smith Wigglesworth on Faith

Smith Wigglesworth on Healing

Smith Wigglesworth on Power to Serve

Smith Wigglesworth on Spirit-Filled Living

Smith Wigglesworth on Spiritual Gifts

Smith Wigglesworth on the Holy Spirit

Wigglesworth on the Anointing